Bird Dog

THE INSTINCTIVE TRAINING METHOD

Ben O. Williams

Willow Creek® PRESS

Published by
Willow Creek Press
P.O. Box 147
Minocqua, Wisconsin 54548

For more information on Willow Creek Press books
and calendars, call 1-800-850-9453.

Design: Todd & Carole Sauers

Library of Congress Cataloguing-in-Publication Data
Williams, Ben O.
    Bird dog : the instinctive training method / Ben O.
Williams.
        p. cm.
    ISBN 1-57223-580-2 (softcover : alk. paper)
    1. Bird dogs--Training. I. Title.
SF428.5 .W55 2002
636.752--dc21

                                        2002009387

Printed in the U.S.A.

DEDICATION

To all the bird dogs I have owned.

ACKNOWLEDGMENTS

I wrote this book for people looking for an easier
and more pleasant way to achieve their personal goals
of what they want in a bird dog. But the most
important acknowledgments go to Darren Brown and
Andrea Donner for their help in photo setups that
better illustrate the text, and for their efforts to help
me expound on my philosophy and training method.

Contents

PART THREE: THE CLASSROOM

PART FOUR: PREP SCHOOL

PART FIVE: GRADUATE SCHOOL

Foreword

When I acquired my first bird dog, I stocked up on as much of the available literature as I could before plunging into training. While I learned a great deal from many excellent trainers, I often came away with the idea that my dog wouldn't be an effective bird dog until he was broken to wing and shot, or "whoa-ed" on a dime while running full-bore a hundred yards out; or that I couldn't train him without

Darren Brown and his two fine German shorthaired pointers hunting Huns on the high plains of Montana.

a specially-designed table or a wide variety of training paraphernalia. These books almost invariably presented everything you could have your dog do, rather than winnowing out the superfluous and focusing in on what you and your dog actually need to do to hunt well together.

Ben Williams' training philosophy takes a far simpler yet completely innovative approach. And any bird hunter who has had the pleasure of spending time with Ben and his wonderful dogs can certainly attest to the results.

I knew of Ben Williams' reputation as a bird hunter and dog trainer long before I actually met him. Still, my first day afield with him was a revelation. Not only were his dogs among the best I'd ever seen, but they also hunted seamlessly with Ben and with each other — without the shock collars, constant whistle blowing, or histrionics I often saw with other bird hunters. Watching a half-dozen great-looking bird dogs pour down a far hillside like water seeking the best course, only to freeze one after another, pointing and relocating to pin a running covey of Huns, was a sight I won't soon forget. But there was something else I remember from that day, beyond just seeing consistently great dog work: commands were minimal, corrections almost completely unnecessary.

I, of course, wanted to know how he'd reached this level of understanding and effectiveness with his dogs, particularly with so many on the ground at once. As I recall, he smiled and remarked that they mostly trained themselves — something I found hard to believe at the time, based on all that I had previously learned about bird dogs.

Later, when hunting my own dogs with Ben's, I saw

just what he meant. My two German short-haired pointers are used to backing each other's points, although they aren't often hunted with other dogs. (As there is little chance of my dogs pointing birds before Ben's when they share bird country, there was no doubt they were going to do a lot of backing.) So I was surprised to see my more experienced dog back briefly in response to a point, and then charge by the phalanx of pointing and backing dogs to deliberately blow through the birds. I was mortified, as I'd just finished telling Ben that my dogs backed without fail. Ben, however, just chuckled. It didn't bother him at all.

Rather than running across the field to chastise the dog, I tried Ben's advice to just watch closely and let the dog work it out for himself. After several more points were made — and several more point-stealing flushes — we could see him becoming more comfortable, creeping cautiously up to join the rest of the backing dogs that were relocating but not pushing the birds. It was a perfect example of a situation that I could easily have made worse by intervening. Instead, the dog learned a valuable lesson about working with other dogs in a relaxed and positive environment. It was quite a lesson for me as well.

I wish to heck I could have read this book before ever heading afield with a dog.

Darren Brown
Editor, *For the Love of a Dog*

Introduction

The first time I got to hunt with Ben was via a sideways invitation through our mutual friend, the great writer but only so-so wing shooter, Jim Fergus. (Not that that matters. It's not like it's necessarily a function of character or anything, to be a good wing shooter. It's just grace, is all. I'm not at all envious of those who have it.) So Ben didn't know what he was getting into. Jim said he'd sideways-invited me because I'm the only person he knows who shoots worse than he does. I don't follow his logic — why saddle Ben and his incredible dogs with two horrid shooters, a plague of poor shooters? But I sure didn't argue.

Rick Bass, author of Brown Dog of the Yaak, *hunting Point-Man for sharp-tailed grouse.*

As Ben mentions in this book, he likes to hunt with his own dogs, line-bred across nearly sixty years for this one landscape, and its two main species of upland birds, Huns and sharptails. He generally doesn't care to throw other dogs onto his playing field. He loves where he is, doing what he's doing, with his own dogs, and coaching and training — and learning from — them. Why should he want some other visitor-dog in his life?

I didn't know that. I showed up at his front porch with my beloved little Point-Man, a Yaak savage par excellence — a whirling, baying, leg-humping, scent-marking, spotted dervish. Two days before I had left on our journey, Point had been sprayed by a skunk — all right, I'll say it, he had pointed the skunk, then charged into the dogwood and seized it by the neck and shook it, whirling around and around in his devil-circle while I fell backwards, trying to evade the slinging spray of skunk-mist — and though I'd doused Point afterward with my unpatented miracle de-odorizer, enough so that he was able to ride the 650 miles to Ben's house sitting in the front seat, in my lap, helping me steer, with only the faintest trace of skunkiness left (really, you'd almost have to know that's what had happened to him, to figure out what the smell was), he was still pretty much completely blind, his beautiful luminous lantern-green eyes now seared an old man's sightless milky-blue, from where the skunk-venom had belted and burned him point-blank.

My vet had said his vision would return, but that it might be a few days, and he had given me some salve, which would help, although since dogs' eye ducts are connected directly to their olfactory systems (as if they literally "see" with their noses, just as we always suspected), it would be a little harder for Point to make game, with the gunky, gacky smell of the poultice flooding his nasal passages. "He might bump a few birds he'd ordinarily have nailed," said Doug, my vet, "but, you know, it's hunting season, it's what he lives for, you can't keep him from it."

I'm trying to get around to the part about what a gentleman Ben is. But you need to understand the image of the couple that arrived at his and his wife's, Bobbie's front door, that beautiful, October, Yellowstone River dusk.

Ben and his wife Bobbie welcomed both Point and me like prodigal sons. Fergus was already there, and my bald-tired, mufflerless, battered truck looked out of place next to his Airstream immaculata (Jim was busy leveling it with a carpenter's tool, shimming it to be just so, ever-so-precise), just as, the next day, my duct-taped, pawn-shop shotgun would look out of place next to Jim's and Ben's fine weaponry. From time to time on the hunt, I would sense them both studying my old blunderbuss — wondering, perhaps, if it had some sentimental value.

One of the finest sportsmen I've ever known, Ben shoots only about one sage grouse every several years, concerned about their population and habitat decline, and he and Bobbie fixed it for us that evening. It was delicious, made more so, somehow, by the fact that his great old dog Winston (who might well have pointed that bird the previous fall) was allowed into the house, in honor of his age and his greatness. And that evening, Point slept in my guest room, and Henri, Sweetz, and Betty with Jim, in his. I know less about dog training, really, than I do about shooting well, but just as I can identify a fine gun by sight, so too are the effects of fine dog training easily observed, and it pleased me immensely to see that Ben's and Jim's excellent dogs did not suffer from being loved deeply, and that indeed, it seemed certain that one of the reasons they excelled was because of it.

I stayed up reading until about midnight, excited for my opportunity, and for Point's. I dreamed of greatness for him.

The next morning we were up early. Ben fixed us a quick breakfast, hinting more than once that we'd need it, that there was plenty of walking in store for us.

Maybe it was a banner year for birds, an epic year, or maybe Ben the gentleman just took us to all his favorite honey-holes that splendid day; I'll never know. All I know is that, true to his word, he walked our butts off, and true to one's dreams, there were birds everywhere we turned: Huns and sharpies. And we followed them all day, on foot, to the horizon and beyond. Ben was twice our age, but he led the way, all day, up and down coulees and ravines, striding briskly.

Ben hardly ever shoots birds any more, he says, but let me tell you, when he lifts his gun and points, the bird falls.

It was not this way for Jim and me.

What I remember of that halcyon day are Ben's Brittanys, six or eight of them on point, five minutes into the hunt, with the October morning sun just risen. Jim and I strode in nervously, disconcerted by having found game so soon. Bam bam, Bass whiffs, Bam bam, Fergus whiffs — mild oaths, brief dog frenzy — and then Ben, who has watched the unscathed covey clatter over the hill, says, cheerfully, "Okay boys, let's go get 'em" — thrilled, I realize now, by our misses, in that the more missing we do, the more hunting his dogs can do. The Bass-and-Fergus shooting school of point-and-release.

I'm not being quite fair. By mid-morning (the three of us sweat-lathered), Jim has hit a bird. Ben was more interested in photographing things than shooting, though sometimes when a covey rise flared in his direction he would lift his lovely little gun, point it very seriously and calmly at one bird or another, and say, very quietly, Bang, you're dead — though he never fired, and the bird kept flying.

My gun really is hideous. For the first five or ten years of this passion, I kept hoping one of the fancy gun companies would comp me the use of some sweet firearm, so that I might then write glowingly of it, should it prove its mettle. It took a while before I realized that the word was already out — I couldn't shoot my way out of a paper bag — and no self-respecting firearm manufacturer would want their product seen anywhere near my inept hands. And often, during this lovely hunt, Ben — ever the professional — would ask if I would turn my gun to the other side, away from the camera's lens. Celebrating beauty, in all that he does; abhorring ugly.

On and on we hunted. I never dreamed I'd see eight or ten dogs honoring point, but it happened again and again that day with Ben. On one particularly exciting pursuit, the birds were scurrying ahead of us so that the dogs leap-frogged one another, honoring each other until they realized the birds had relocated, at which point a Number Two or Three dog would surge to the front — everyone would freeze up again — before the ex-Number One dog surged back to the front — freeze — only to then be trumped by the Number Six or Seven dog.

How our hearts survived it, I'll never know, and when the birds finally held, and we flushed them, there was nothing left to us but adrenaline and spirit, and we missed, pow pow, pow pow, but I have never seen anything like it, and will never forget it. . .

Each time we missed, Ben made us go after the departing flock, a stern taskmaster. The coveys flew farther with each flush, and glided still farther, and Ben loved it, exercising the dogs, the birds, and the hapless hunters, all bright and exceedingly alive, that day, on the canvas of his vast and beloved home landscape.

Eventually, we got a few more birds, and, looking back on it, these many years later, I suppose I have to concede in my heart of hearts that they were probably all Jim's — all three of them. But at the time, I was not so sure, because usually — like wolves selecting the weak or infirm — our guns would swing on the same bird: the straggler, the trailer, the flare-away solo. And we'd shoot at pretty much the same time, and occasionally, that bird would go down, at which point one of Ben's crisp dogs would go retrieve it.

We were pretty gentlemanly about such occurrences at first — as if spellbound beneath Ben's magnanimous influence — but as the day progressed and we grew hot and tired, it seemed to me that Jim began to grow a little curt with me whenever I'd say, "Oh, finally, I got one," or, "I can't believe I finally hit one!" ("I can't either," I thought I heard Jim mutter once.)

You might be wondering how little Skunk Man performed. Let's just say that he was not at the top of his game, and leave it at that. His heart was big though, that day, even if his skunked-out nose wasn't. On the few occasions that I had him down on the ground with Ben's dogs, he would thunder past them the instant one of the other dogs went on point. Often in that hilly country they would be pointing a covey just on the other side of a low rise, and it became a familiar sight to see Point rocketing past the other dogs and crossing that rise as if it were some marathoner's long-desired finish line.

There'd be a few excited yips, and by the time we came

over the rise a couple minutes later, there'd be nothing but space and sky, as if Point had been swallowed by the void. I didn't have a check cord for him, and tried to fashion one out of my belt, but he kept pulling free and charging off, the belt flapping behind him. At that point, if I'd had a metal pot with a coonskin cap, I could have put it on and worn it for a cap, the only thing lacking to fully complete the picture; but instead, I finally retired Point for the day, apologizing to Ben and Jim and Ben's and Jim's dogs. Ben didn't mind, and said that his dogs didn't either. "They're gentlemen," he said nonchalantly — as if they saw such things every day. As if he had tutored them in how to respond.

Ben's great gentlemanliness extends, of course, beyond the world of humans and into the realm of dog land, whose rules and codes are at least as mysterious as our own. Honor-driven yet forgiving, it is a wonderful realm to inhabit or even visit, and what I think I like best about Ben's training methods is that they key on one of the greatest and most refined strengths of any dog, which is the desire to please. And like all great dog trainers, Ben reminds us that the dog is almost never wrong — maybe not always right, but never really wrong — and that any failures, or perceived failures, are our own responsibility.

Much of what you'll read in this book will seem to counter some things you might have read in previous years, by other trainers. Some of it, such as letting pointing dogs "creep," or even steal a point, will seem revolutionary. Some of the advice is refreshingly straightforward, and yet not always heard, or heeded, like Ben's repeated counsel for both the dog and the hunter to have fun.

I've had the privilege of hanging around some of the finest dog trainers in the world. All of them are precise, patient, soothing, gentle, and firm with their dogs. The best ones love what they do, and have an abiding respect for dogs. I don't mean they just like or love dogs, I mean they respect, to the point of marvel, the dogs' abilities and various temperaments. There is nothing that dogs do that such trainers do not find wonderful. Some of these masters' training methods might differ quite a bit from Ben's, and, for each trainer's specific set of dogs, and specific quarry, and specific landscape, his or her other training method might work like a dream. I think what this points out, however, is that it is, as Ben reiterates, the responsibility of the trainer, not the dog, to do the right thing.

I love, too, how Ben seems to distinguish, with utmost patience, between "mistakes" of enthusiasm, versus mistakes of disobedience, while acknowledging, again, that the initial source of any mistakes almost always lies with the trainer, not the dog.

Having seen other fine trainers work, and then having seen Ben work, I think that there are different ways to do the right thing. Hardly a revolutionary concept. And yet when I remember that whiffing day afield with Ben and Jim, and the magisterial nature of the dog work, I think that indeed there might be something revolutionary after all about what Ben is proposing here, and about his sixty years of quiet patience in the field.

Never run to your dog on point, he counsels here. It's ineffective, as well as perhaps just plain undignified. Jim and I hadn't read his book that October day, and so we were hauling up and down those hills like sprinters, all day long. (Ben was too gentlemanly to point out the folly of our ways; and what did it matter, really?)

Ben stayed with us, somehow, without having to ever run — truth be told, he walked the shoeleather off us

— but one of the images I have from that amazing day is Jim and I, flushed and breathless, hurrying up yet another steep knoll toward the waiting dogs.

I looked back for some reason — rare, in the heat of the hunt, for me to pause like that — and was surprised to see that Ben had stopped on the ridge above us, and was just standing there, gun broken and folded in his arms, and was watching us and the dogs, and he was smiling: just standing there grinning — not caring whether we got to the birds in time or not, not caring if we hit or missed, or if one of the Brittanys released and scooched up a bit.

From his vantage, everything had already gone perfectly, and couldn't be improved upon. He'd spent sixty years sculpting a big-running but gentle and obedient dog with a heart like a lion and a nose like a fox. There were still birds on his beloved prairie, gloriously wild birds, and his dogs — not always perfect, but always true and passionate — had gone out and found them.

In that looking-back glimpse, I've rarely seen a man look happier, or more contented. I think that satisfaction, that kindness and respect, will shine through between the lines of this book, and it is an image I try to remember always, with my own dogs, in all landscapes, and all the years.

Rick Bass

Point Bass' Miracle Skunk Deodorizer

One gallon warm water
half cup dishwashing detergent
16 oz. hydrogen peroxide
quarter-cup of baking soda

Mix together in jug or bucket until soapy, then knead into dog's coat. Odor will vanish within minutes.

Part One: Getting Started

A HUNTING DOG PHILOSOPHY

This book shares a philosophy that takes the complexity out of training and dispels the myth that it takes a professional trainer to make a hunting dog. This method is about letting the dog be a dog in the field instead of being a canine robot. This is not a step-by-step, how-to training manual that promotes methods like force breaking, or anything else that plays no part in developing a dog's natural instincts. The natural training method I use develops a dog's innate abilities, utilizes the animal's genes, and develops companionship to achieve upland hunting bliss, so that when the hunting day is over, both you and your dog have had an enjoyable experience.

Eliza Frazier with Shoe taking a break after hunting Huns.

This book eliminates so-called routine training practices and drills that are unnecessary. It is not about training a dog to become the envy of a prestigious hunting club, nor is it about training a dog to become a field-trial champion. It is written for the person who has a bird dog — or is thinking of buying one — and wants a companion, both in the field and at home. It contains my philosophy of how man and dog should work together to achieve camaraderie while hunting upland game birds. This method is for the hunter who wants to learn a safe, easy way to handle a dog while enjoying the process, and accepting the mistakes made by both parties. It's about man and dog achieving excellence in its simplest form.

My dogs are bird dogs, but they are definitely a part of my family. My philosophy and the training method I use will work for a puppy or an older dog, whether it lives in the house or is kept in a kennel. This method will also work if you only hunt 10 days or so a year, be it on a preserve or on wild lands. But the more days you and your dog get in the field, the better both of you will be for it.

All you need to make this method of training work for you is common sense, dedication, camaraderie, and a little time. The reward is well worth it.

HUNTER AND COMPANION

Like humans, dogs have always been hunters. Genetic studies using DNA have shown that dogs evolved from wolves, and at the molecular level dogs still remain similar to their ancestors, even though there are many different physical characteristics within the hundreds of modern breeds.

Dale and Lila Critz resting Hershey after a hot morning of grouse hunting.

Fossil evidence suggests that around twelve thousand years ago, humans appear to have accepted the presence of wolves around their camps. Whether they adopted pups and domesticated them or whether wolves domesticated themselves by moving closer to camp to scavenge leftover food is unknown. Either way, it was the wolf's intelligence and ability to adapt that made it a permanent partner in the lives of hunter-gatherers.

The wolf's social structure revolves around the pack. The pack's size can be as small as two or may number over ten, depending on the size of the prey they target. Pack animals have a strict hierarchy, which we call a "pecking order." This hierarchy is complex and subtle, but in simple terms, the strongest male and his mate (the alpha male and female) are the dominant wolves. Dominance is established by the submission of weaker males during confrontation. Every wolf knows its place in the descending pecking order, but younger members in the pack are constantly challenging for higher status. Although this social structure is one of dominance, it also helps the pack work together for food and protection. All of their activities are coordinated by the pack, and each wolf understands the intentions of other members so the pack can work together as one unit. Young wolves learn from older, more experienced wolves, and all able-bodied members participate in hunting for food. The alpha male eats first, the rest in the order of dominance. Any member left behind during the hunting expedition, such as a mother wolf with pups, is provided with food brought back by the pack.

Over time, domesticated wolf-like canines were developed into human-friendly dogs of many sizes and shapes. Being highly intelligent, they became useful in assisting man. Through the millennia, dogs have been bred for hunting, battle, work, assisting the disabled, and as companions. Once domesticated, dogs became loyal to their masters, but in return they also became dependent on man.

The more we study wolves the more we are able to understand dogs. The behavior of dominance that wolves display is still inherent in all domestic dog breeds. So is predatory behavior like stalking, pointing, backing, chasing, flushing, herding, digging for prey, killing, and retrieving. The instinct of the alpha wolf to bring food back to the mother's

Rupert Colemore with one of his many fine red dogs (Irish setters).

den manifests itself today in gun dogs that naturally retrieve birds for us, and in puppies that love to carry things around.

WHO IS IN CHARGE?

My dogs are pack animals, but they feel content in knowing that I am in command. They respond to and respect their pack leader much like wolves do. To them, comfort and survival depends on me, the alpha dog, and this is why they are willing to obey. To a dog, survival means food and this is true throughout its life. That is why training goes on continuously

I establish my leadership role from the moment each dog or pup arrives. Every dog knows its place, but the positions are constantly being challenged within my pack of dogs. (Just watch two dogs meet for the first time and you will see that they quickly establish who is dominant.) This idea of dominance is the fundamental key to training all dogs.

UNDERSTANDING YOUR DOG'S SENSES

In training, human knowledge of a canine's sensory capabilities and native language is as important as a dog understanding our own system of communication. Thoroughly understand how your dog gathers and uses information, and learning for both of you will become much easier.

Dogs think in a logical way, yet nothing like we do. Their logic is much simpler than ours, and a large proportion of a dog's brain is used for sensory perception. They are attuned to subtle changes in their world that we often cannot recognize, leading us to think that they possess a kind of sixth sense at times.

Even with snow on the ground, this pointer is locked up on birds. We cannot comprehend a pointing dog's sense of smell.

For a sporting dog, the sense of smell monopolizes the brain, and the nose is a good portion of the head. Their noses are literally packed with scent receptors. Dogs have over 250 million receptors compared to about 20 million receptors in humans. Their sense of smell is so much more powerful than ours that we cannot really comprehend how they perceive or recognize the world around them.

Throughout history, humans have utilized this incredible sense of smell to help find birds, mammals, and other people. In favorable scenting conditions (good moisture and wind), I've had dogs pick up bird scent two hundred yards away. I cannot even get close to their kennels without them knowing it.

A dog also has acute hearing that is remarkably superior to ours. They can hear high frequencies, which allows them to hear some things long before we do. It is estimated that a dog's hearing is five times greater than ours—meaning they can hear sounds five times quieter and five times farther away than we can.

Anyone who spends a lot of time around dogs sees just how attuned they become to small cues. Hershey and Winston, two of my permanent house dogs, stay in the office when I'm writing on my computer. When I quit working, I always make a backup copy of the file on a floppy disk. The sound of the disk running alerts the dogs to the fact that I'm finished, and they get up from their nap, go to the door, and stand ready to leave with me.

Dogs see the world differently than we do too. One reason is the location of their eyes. A hunting dog has excellent peripheral vision (field of vision) and can see up to 260 degrees, but their binocular vision (looking straight ahead) is poor. Also, dogs do not see colors like we do, although they can see much better in the dark than humans. While a dog's vision is much more blurry than ours, they can detect the faintest movements immediately, no matter how far away or in low light.

Once, while hunting chukars, I put two dogs on the ground and before I could get my gun out of the pickup, both Brittanys were sight pointing. Their heads were held high toward a ridgetop three hundred yards away. I knew they were not pointing scent because the wind was screaming down through the canyon at their backs. After a minute, I made out several small objects running on the ground. I did not realize they were chukars until they flushed and flew over the ridge. The dogs had spotted the movement long before I did.

A dog's sense of taste is far less acute than ours. It is probably the least important of their senses. They are worried more about filling their bellies than about the kind of food they eat. As a dog's nose is a thousand times more sensitive than its taste buds, they eat more by smell than taste. As all of us know, dogs eat things that are very repulsive to us, like a dead fish found on the bank of a river, but it smells good to them so they eat it.

Maybe a dog's true sixth sense is its "native tongue." Dogs communicate with each other and us, even though we may not recognize their language. They converse by scent and body language. Facial expressions like yawning, or gestures of greeting, aggression, fear, submission, and dominance are all part of a dog's native tongue.

Dogs, and most animals, are very sensitive to barometric pressure, which alerts them to changes in the weather. Dogs also sense daily changes in their owners. They can recognize when we are sick or depressed, when we are leaving for a trip, or other happenings around the house of which we think they are unaware Just start packing your hunting clothes, load up the vehicle, and watch how your dog responds. If I happen to get upset while working on a piece of lawn equipment, for instance, and a couple dogs are with me, they immediately sense that something is wrong and become nervous. Their extraordinary senses allow them to tune-in to small nuances in their environment, whether around the house or in the field.

Understanding how dogs use their senses and how they communicate is vital to "reading" a dog during training.

PEOPLE AND DOGS

There are people who hunt upland game birds with no dogs at all, but this is not the best way to do it. Not having a bird dog along when hunting birds is like eating Thanksgiving turkey without dressing and gravy.

You can do without, but it takes a lot of the pleasure out of the experience.

There are dog owners who yell and scream, continuously blow a training whistle, and give hand signals to no avail that still believe their dogs are completely under control. Others become frustrated and angry in the field because their dogs are not responding to their commands. Some over-train, making the dog's experience monotonous instead of fun, and others let their dogs self-hunt and run free without any training whatsoever.

Of course, the real level of excellence a dog attains in the field is in the eye of the owner, but negative situations result when people do not have a true understanding of what a dog is all about. The joy in hunting should be shared by both the hunter and the dog, and it is up to each individual owner to determine what level of obedience their hunting companion will achieve.

Tracy Lee and Scotty Searle walk slowly past Perk, the trailing pointer, who is backing the other dogs. The lead Brittany has a covey of Huns locked down.

Perk Perkins, President of The Orvis Company, has had bird dogs all his life. While hunting with my Brittany, Winston, and pointer, Rip, he feels right at home.

For the non-dog owner who hunts, there is a different perspective. Many have no idea what to expect of a hunting dog and become critical or give commands when hunting with someone else and their dog, thinking that they are being helpful. A hunter may feel that a friend's dog seemingly lacks any formal training, but it's the owner's jurisdiction to shape the animal's performance. Whether you are a dog owner or not, it's important to remember that a dog has only one master at a time. One dog, one voice.

CHOOSING A BREED FOR YOUR HUNTING NEEDS

Hunters have depended on dogs for thousands of years. Today, gun dogs are some of the most trustworthy breeds in the world. There are over 50 distinct gun dog breeds that are generally lumped into three categories: retrievers, flushers, and pointers.

As we are all individuals, my choice of a gun dog and yours will likely be different. It so happens that I prefer the pointing breeds, even though I have had several good retrievers. To me, it is still magical every time a dog locks up on point. The information in this book is about communicating with your dog, and while it is certainly slanted more for the pointing breeds, I believe it will serve you well no matter what breed of gun dog you own.

Pointing breeds became an integral part of the North American hunting scene during the latter part of the

During this training session, seven dogs back and honor the lead dog. They stand rock-solid until we arrive. Six are my Brittanys and the other two are Darren Brown's shorthaired pointers.

A "shooting pointer," Rip retrieves a moment after Tom Petrie dumped a full-grown Hun.

1800s. These dogs were highly specialized and extremely efficient for hunting certain upland game birds.

Not everyone agrees about what a pointing dog should do in the field, and there are two main schools of thought. The "classic pointer" searches out game birds and solidly stops and points from far enough away to hold the birds. The dog stands rock-solid until the hunter arrives, then the hunter walks past the dog, flushes the birds, and shoots the game while the dog holds "steady to wing and shot." Then the hunter commands the dog to retrieve. This type of performance by a finished dog can be impressive to watch. Usually, this is a field-trial dog or a specialist that focuses on just one bird, such as bobwhite quail, but this is not always what an average bird hunter wants in a pointer.

A "shooting pointer" is likely going to hunt many

I do not train dogs to be steady to wing and shot. Here, my dogs have worked a covey of Huns. Each time the hunter passes the dogs on point, they relocate and point again. But this time the birds flush a bit out of range. The hunter made the right decision by not shooting.

species of game birds over its life span and it works a little differently. The "shooting pointer" still searches out game birds and solidly points and holds the birds until the hunter arrives, but some hunters flush the birds themselves, while others walk in with the dog to flush the birds. These pointers are not steady to wing and shot, but they are in a better position to fetch birds or catch cripples that might otherwise escape. Take your pick. How you train your dog is up to you, as all the pointing breeds will respond to either method.

Within the pointing breeds, the English pointer, usually just called a pointer, and the English setter are usually used solely for pointing and retrieving upland game birds, and have the longest history of doing so in this country. But in the past 50 years, the versatile pointing dog, or general-purpose gun dog, has grown in popularity in the United States.

These dogs are used for hunting game from the northern woodlands to the southern swamps, and from the farmlands of the Midwest to the open prairies of the West. Rare is the urban wingshooter these days who

English setters have a lot of class when they point. This big hard-running dog has just found a big bunch of prairie chickens.

can afford the luxury of having a number of bird dogs for different kinds of hunting. Versatile pointing dogs allow modern hunters to pursue different types of game with one dog. Versatile breeds include the Brittany, German short-haired pointer, and German wirehaired pointer, among others.

The versatile dog does essentially the same thing as the pointer and setter while hunting upland game birds, but it also performs well as a waterfowl and tracking dog. Understand, though, that of the many versatile pointing dogs, ability and style vary greatly, not only between the breeds but also among dogs from different breeders.

MAKE A SELECTION TO FIT YOUR LIFESTYLE

Many factors go into the selection of a gun dog. You must consider the principal game you plan to hunt, physical characteristics of the terrain, and the climate in which you live. Owning a dog involves a good deal of commitment, so you'll also need to consider how much time you're willing to spend with your dog.

You probably have already been influenced by several outside factors that are not necessarily helpful in choosing a dog. For instance, things like the popularity of a breed, eye appeal, and fondness for a breed you had as a child are not part of a systematic approach to

choosing the right breed. Your initial concern should involve what you expect the dog to do in the field. Bear in mind that each breed hunts a little differently. Some breeds are generally big-running dogs, while others are close-working. Some breeds take more time than others to train, and there are also variations in range and temperament within a specific breed. I've had some great bird dogs over the years, and when everything goes right, training is easy. I also know that things don't always go that way, and many more hours of training are needed for some individual dogs.

David Guterson, author of Snow Falling on Cedars, *waits for his hunting partner before he flushes the birds. Owning a pointing dog takes a commitment, but the end result is that they will pay you back many times over.*

THOUGHTS ON GETTING A NEW PUP

If you are thinking about getting your first hunting dog, you probably haven't the foggiest notion of how to locate a quality dog. First, I recommend thoroughly reading periodicals and surfing Internet sites that cover the different kinds of hunting dogs. *The Encyclopedia of Sporting Dogs*, for which I am a co-author, is a good place to start and provides valuable

I'm not sure who is the happier, Cole Claiborn or Red, a Brittany pup. In a year, both are in for some good hunting.

information and helpful tips in making the right choice.

After accumulating facts on each breed, you will be ready to start looking for a hunting partner. Your first thought may be to find a pup locally or within a short distance of home, but this is not always the best approach. It's a lot safer to buy a pup from a reliable, established breeder than to get one from a backyard breeder who thinks his dog Rex is the best hunting dog since shotguns were invented. It is a good idea to check the classified ads in the major sporting magazines and on the Internet to get a feel for major kennels and breeders. Today, checking on a reputable breeder is quite simple. A good breeder will send you pertinent information about their breeding program and personal references from folks that have their dogs.

Over the years, hunting dogs have greatly improved,

thanks to many of today's outstanding breeders. I would not hesitate to buy a pup over the phone from a reliable breeder. In fact, I recently did just that, ordering two new pups from different breeders to strengthen the female side of my bloodlines.

PICK THE PARENTS, NOT THE PUP

Maybe the first dog you owned was a great hunting dog. Maybe you found it in the classified ads in your local newspaper and picked the pup up across town. The pup's mother was friendly, and the owner said she was a good hunter. He also told you that the male was owned by a hunting buddy, but he hadn't hunted it much. Your dog may have been a German shorthaired pointer that was a weekend warrior and

This female red dog (Irish setter) is an outstanding bird finder. The best way to pick a pup is to look at the parents. At this point in time, I believe she would rather be bird hunting.

the envy of a Texas quail hunting club. Or maybe it was a high-tailed English setter that shook down every piece of brush in your favorite grouse covert. But if it was, you got lucky.

The best way to pick a pup is to look at the parents. When you know the heredity of the parents, their field performance and conformation, the odds of getting a good hunting companion greatly increase.

Heredity is easily tracked on the dog's pedigree, but I'm not always impressed with a long list of titles. A dog's performance in the field gets my attention though. Conformation, by definition, is the manner of formation, structure, and adaptation — the orderly arrangement of its parts. But in the dog world, two considerations apply: stationary (static) conformation and functional (kinetic) conformation. Static conformation applies more to standing posture, while kinetic applies more to body movement, running gear, and gait. I'm not sure that the two can be separated in the hunting breeds, even though I look more for functional conformation.

If possible, take a hard look at the parents' actual hunting abilities. Better yet, look at parents that have already had a litter of pups. This makes it possible to check out the previous litter or litters to see how well the offspring of this male/female combination have done in the field. My experience, and I believe this holds true everywhere, is that if all the pups in any one litter are good, the next breeding with the same parents will also be good. You may find the best sire and dam in the country, but in and of itself, that does not guarantee that together they will produce a great litter, even though the chances are better than with a completely random combination.

If you pick a reputable breeder with strong bloodlines that traditionally produces good litters, you'll get a good pup.

PICKING A PUP FROM THE LITTER

No matter what you read or hear, the chances of picking the most outstanding hunter from a litter of pups is about the same as hitting the jackpot on a slot machine — it's more luck than ability. Is the pup bold? Is it the first to find the mother's nipple and feed? Does the pup come running at the first sign of people? Will the pup point a dangled bird wing? Will the pup jump if a door is slammed or a food dish banged? Is the pup shy of people? And on and on it goes.

I can tell you exactly how to pick a female from a male, or how to pick the biggest pup in the litter, or

Which Brittany pup would you pick out of this litter?

The versatile German wirehaired pointer has recently gained in popularity. Pick a reputable breeder with strong bloodlines that traditionally produces good litters and you can't go wrong.

the one with the most interesting color and markings. Beyond that, my advice is to pick the pup that looks the best to you or just have the breeder make the choice.

I've owned well over a hundred dogs, mostly pups from my Brittany breeding bloodlines, but I've also owned pointers, English setters, and Labs from other reliable breeders. Most of my dogs have been good, and I've also had my share of great dogs. Two of the earliest were female pups with outstanding parents. As I already had a great male, I started with good stock, select-bred, and developed pups with desire, trainability, and big hearts. The parents were smart, had good breed conformation, and were high-legged with hard-driving wheels. Once I found the right male/female combination, I stuck with it because every pup had the potential to become a good gun dog. After the first litter, I kept several pups from subsequent litters, and I found it impossible to predict the most outstanding pup. They were almost carbon copies of each other.

Later, using the same breeding, I gave buyers the first choice and kept the last pup of the litter. One of these pups, named Shoe, became my leading stud dog. My point is that even though every pup out of this breeding had potential, picking the best hunter was like playing poker: "You pays your money and you takes your chances."

PUP OR OLDER DOG

The material in this book is directed to the person who is interested in getting a pup or who has just bought a new pup, but that doesn't mean this philosophy of training dogs will not apply to working with an older dog. I have never supported the old adage, "You can't teach an old dog new tricks." A dog can learn at any age, and even a dog that has never learned can still be taught. Learning is an ongoing process throughout a dog's life. I've had several dogs of different breeds that were still untrained at two to three years old that became good bird dogs when finally given the chance. No matter what the age, if a dog is smart, it will learn quickly.

One dog I had, Mike, was a big dog. Even though the veterinarian showed me his pedigree papers, he looked more like a red-and-white setter than a Brittany, with ears that seemed too high on his head. His owner did not have the time to train him so he let him run free, and Mike became a street fighter. Every dog in the neighborhood respected him. Mike was extremely friendly to people, especially the dogcatcher, with whom he spent a great deal of time.

With Mike spending more time at the pound than at home and with neighbors regularly complaining, his owner finally had enough and quit paying the city dog pound bills. After a month of no payments, Mike was sent to the city veterinarian. The owner was told to pay the bill and get the dog out of town or they would have him put down. However, the veterinarian took a liking to Mike and thought he was worth saving.

He knew I had Brittanys and gave me a call. I agreed to try the dog, and if he didn't work out I could return him. I called the owner and asked about Mike. He was delighted I had taken the dog but warned me Mike had had no obedience training. He said Mike spent a great deal of time chasing deer, antelope, jackrabbits, and running pheasants, which to me was not unusual for a good, untrained bird dog. It seems that Mike's idea of hunting was to run hard, hunt long, and return to the pickup after dark for a ride home. Of course, this wasn't the owner's idea of a hunting dog. Before he put the phone down, the previous owner wished me luck.

Mike was over two years old when I got him. He accepted the routine of kennel life and got along surprisingly well with the other Brittanys. In fact, he enjoyed being around the dogs and responded well to controlled discipline. Mike wasn't hard-headed, and after a few verbal attitude adjustments and after being exposed to lots of birds in the field, he forgot about running down his furry friends.

Mike would sweep the big, open country and if there were any gray partridge within his range, he'd find them, lock up, and never move until I arrived. He became a master at working the big wheatfields of the West. To this day, I've had only a few dogs that could cover that much ground. Mike is just one example of a dog that came from a good background whose breeding proved itself in the right conditions with the right handling, despite the fact that he wasn't trained as a pup.

If a dog has the breeding and the desire to hunt, age is not important. It's the time you spend with him in the field that counts. Like any athletic endeavor, the more time spent practicing the better one becomes. Picking an older hunting dog also has some advantages. For one thing, there's little doubt about what the dog will look like and what its personality will be. The downside may be in having to break some bad habits.

A BREEDING PROGRAM

Canines have a lot more chromosomes than humans; dogs have 78, humans have 64. With this number of chromosomes, and due to the fact that dogs mature fast and can reproduce at a young age, we have the opportunity to selectively breed certain features into a bloodline within a very short period of time.

I've developed dogs with an instinctive natural ability to point, back, and retrieve. . . and also to be friendly to other dogs. This German shorthaired is reluctant to get a drink, but he had a great time bunting with my pack of dogs.

While I've owned a variety of breeds, I've been breeding a special line of Brittanys for over 40 years, and have produced many generations of dogs. I've developed dogs with an instinctive natural ability to point, back, and retrieve. Not only did I breed for instinctive traits, I created big, strong-running dogs with a predominantly white coat. My primary goals were to have animals that had natural hunting ability, could cover lots of country over long periods, and had coats that could be seen easily at a great distance. These days, seeing a dog in the field is less important because sound, through the use of electronic beeper collars, can replace sight as a way to stay in contact. As a result, the color white has not been a serious criterion in my breeding program for the past several years.

I mainly breed dogs for my own use, and my bloodlines are geared first and foremost for hunting all species of wild upland game birds in North America, even though I spend most of my time hunting and training on prairie game birds in the big, open country of the West.

I trained Brittanys part-time for Oberlin Kennels in northern Illinois during my college years, and I got my first two females from there when I moved west. A couple of years later, I bought a male from Mr. Oberlin sight-unseen, but knowing him and his kennels, I had confidence in getting a good dog. Back in those days pups were shipped by train, and that dog was one scared pup when he arrived. (You might recognize his field name, Michael McGillicuddy, as he was written about extensively.) McGilly became an outstanding gun dog while still in his first year in the field. He pointed, honored other dogs by backing, and retrieved naturally, with no force training. He was not a big-running dog, but he sure found birds.

When McGilly was three, I purchased two field-trial,

horseback-style female Brittanys from Jim Leverick's Tip Top Kennels in Pampa, Texas. Jim's Brittanys were big-running dogs. Oberlin and Tip Top Kennels had outstanding bloodlines, and the combination of the two lines worked perfectly. The pups were field smart, big running, strong, athletic, and natural hunters — just what I wanted for the wide-open western plains.

My program works like this: I produce a litter of Brittany pups to supplement my kennels and replace aging dogs. (The number of dogs in my kennel averages around 12 to 14.) Replacing older dogs is not the only reason I try to keep one or two young, starter pups around, of course. I also enjoy having a young pup on hand to work with. I sell the surplus pups to bird hunters, folks that spend a lot of time in the field. The dogs are bred for hard hunting, and I do not want any pup to fall into hands that are not going to use them to hunt.

Ben's Dogs

Hershey: A Soft Dog With a Strong Heart

No two dogs are alike; even most littermates have little similarity. Hershey came from a large litter of Brittany pups, and as a pup he was very sensitive to any type of loud commands or forceful training methods. He didn't need any kind of discipline because he always responded quickly when called. Like his father, he was dominant but not aggressive around other male dogs, and when hunting he was all business.

Some folks believe a soft dog will not make a good hunting dog, but being soft has nothing to do with a dog's hunting skills. If I had to make a choice between a hard-headed dog and a soft dog, I would choose the latter. Intelligence genes play more of a part in getting a good bird finder than personality.

At six months, Hershey found his first covey of Huns. It was mid-August and I had been running him alone. Although he remained rock solid until I got there, I could tell he was excited. I stood alongside him for several minutes watching him tremble with emotion before several young birds flushed. I let him chase, never giving him a command to stop. After covering a short distance, he came back quickly and searched the cover from which the birds had flushed, then pointed again. I walked over and praised him, saying "Good dog, good dog." To my surprise, a single Hungarian partridge flushed from under his nose. This time he did not chase but held tight until two more birds flushed nearby.

I have never disciplined Hershey because there has been no need to. A smart dog learns to hunt birds on its own from its genes, not from a trainer. A good bird dog is 95 percent genes and 5 percent training. But, poorly initiated, that training can ruin a soft dog.

My wife Bobbie named Hershey. She called him that because as a pup he was a sweet little thing. And he still is today.

Hershey may be a soft dog around people, but he's dynamite in the bird field.

Part Two:
Home School

DON'T TAKE THE DOG OUT OF THE DOG

I run dogs in the field over two hundred days a year, although not always in shooting or hunting situations. Many times, I take the whole pack out to exercise and just have fun. This lasts only an hour or so. I call it "Dog's Fun Day." I've been asked many times, "Don't you think it's important to shoot over the dogs when you take them hunting?" My answer is, "Nonsense!" The dogs learn that some days we are just out to have

David Guterson slowly walks up to the two pointers and two Brittanys. He knows in a moment the earth is going to explode in a fury of wings.

a run. The truth is, they love to point birds and they don't have to retrieve every bird pointed. Thank goodness, too, as no one I know can shoot every wild bird pointed in the field anyway. I believe that the dogs sense my enjoyment in seeing them point, even if I don't shoot, and they certainly enjoy it themselves. When in a hunting situation, I put two braces of dogs down at a time and run them for two to three hours, then put four more down. I continue hunting until all of the dogs have had a chance to run.

At first, I start a pup with older dogs during the fun sessions. I also work a pup singly in the field. If I have two young dogs, I'll run them together, but I'm very cautious not to let them run free and I make sure they come on command. As a pup gets older, I work it with the older dogs in the field. Let me emphasize one important point: I always have control over all the dogs, no matter how many are down.

Folks have said that the success of my training program is in having lots of dogs. They think that all I have to do is put a pup with the pack and the older

Sometimes a pup just doesn't know what they are supposed to point. Here, a Brittany sight-points a cow!

dogs train the young one. Well, I wish it were that easy, but it's not. After years of observation I will admit that a young pup will gain confidence more rapidly in the field by having more dogs around, but that does not stop a pup from learning on its own. Certainly, pups learn to honor another dog on point by having a dog, or something that resembles another dog, in the field. There is place where I hunt sharp-tailed grouse that has an old white refrigerator at the bottom of a grassy draw. Every time the dogs come to the draw and see the white object they all stop and back the refrigerator, thinking it's a dog on point. When hunting with guests, I often let them think the dogs are pointing birds. It makes for a good story afterwards.

Other than a pup honoring a point in the field, my observations do not support the theory that a pointing dog trains another dog or puppy to point or to hunt. A smart pup learns to hunt birds from its own genes, not from another dog — or a trainer.

TRAINING A BIRD DOG IS NOT A MYSTERY

Companionship is what binds a dog to its owner, and field experience unlocks the best of its genes, allowing it to become a top performer. If you have ever watched a great gun dog in action, regardless of the breed, that bundle of fur is working its heart out to please its hunting companion. A bird dog with excellent genes will offset any dog owner's amateur training skills as long as there is a close camaraderie between the two. A dog wants to do what you want it to, but it first has to decipher what exactly that is. Using common sense and the simplest possible form of communication is the easiest way for both the dog and owner to achieve excellence.

In this book, training is more of a philosophy that dog owners can use to develop their own method of communicating with a dog than a rigid, step-by-step set of rules. Training a bird dog is not mystical or mysterious; it is a simple, planned training process that is ongoing from the first day you receive a new dog.

It takes the dedication of the person and the willingness of the dog to make the process work. The person who has personally gone through the "educational process" with a bird dog will have a more devoted relationship and more meaningful memories of shared experiences.

Let's look at some of the things to think about when a new puppy comes home with you.

THE PUP'S EARLY LEARNING

Now that you have made the decision on the kind of breed you want and picked the kennel, it is time to pick up the new baby. If this is your first pup, the experience may be an awakening. Every new pup that I have chosen, whether it was from my own female's litter or someone else's, has been a new and different experience, but the end results are invariably rewarding.

Getting a pup is an investment, but more importantly, that dog is going to become a part of your life and your family's life. Once you make the selection and have the registration papers and health records in your pocket, your commitment is going to last 10 to 15 years. I must say, though, that I've had two or more bird dogs for most of my life, and I wouldn't trade one minute of it.

While my role with my dogs is one of authority, it is also one of respect, companionship, and cama-

raderie. In the early stages of the pup's life in the field, you are the instructor. As time progresses, the learning curve flattens out and is shared by both of you. Later still, the confidence in your hunting companion grows to the point that you will become dependent on him in the field.

The first few days the pup is with you is a critical time and can affect its personality for the rest of its life. At the time you acquire your pup, its behavior has been primarily influenced by its mother and the relationship it had with its littermates. This first week is not a training period but an adjustment period from momma dog to you. The day you pick him up his whole world comes crashing down, so it's your responsibility to make him comfortable and happy through the transition.

Suddenly the pup is whisked away from its littermates and subjected to a scary new environment, usually experiencing motion sickness for the first time in its life before being introduced to entirely new surroundings and a new family.

River and Kessly Lovec play with their new Brittany pups. The more time spent with people, the happier the pup's transition period becomes.

49

If you have another dog and it is receptive to the new arrival, your pup's transition usually becomes much easier. Without another dog in the house, some pups still adjust readily to the abrupt changes in their environment, while other pups may take a long time to become comfortable. Be aware of how your pup is reacting to its new home. Once the puppy has arrived, let him run free and familiarize himself with the new surroundings.

Many breeders feel the best time to acquire a puppy is between seven and nine weeks old. I'm sure it's best for the breeder, but that does not mean an older pup is harder to train. Years ago, when puppies were shipped by trucks or trains instead of airlines, breeders often said the best time to get a pup was when it was at least

German wirehaired pointers. The day you pick up your new pup, its whole world changes. You are now its keeper.

twelve weeks old. Their thinking back then was that a pup should have more time to be with its mother and littermates. There are many similarities between wolves and domestic dogs, and wolf pups spend their entire adolescence with the female and the rest of the pack as they learn.

I'm not sure if anyone really knows the best age to get a pup. A dog's makeup is completely different than a human's. Folks have often said to me, "My dog thinks it's a human." But a dog would never think of itself as human; rather, it sees you as another dog. I have gotten several older pups and adult dogs that have responded as well as any eight-week-old pup. If an older dog has good bloodlines and was not abused when young, the probability of it being a good hunting companion has nothing to do with age. In my experience, an older dog's learning timetable may be a bit longer, but it will come around just as well as a pup.

A dog's manners, routine, and even its personality can change at any age. "Bonding with a dog" is a human expression. I don't believe any domestic animal fully bonds with a human. Perhaps a dog does bond with one person at a time, but if that animal changes homes the bonding usually goes with the dog to the next person who cares for it. I've had a close relationship with every dog I've raised or acquired, but when transferred to a new owner, that dog adapted well no matter what the age — and in a short time.

Respect, appreciation, care, a sense of order, and dominance are what binds a dog to a man. Just look at all the dogs that are successfully adopted from animal shelters that go on to lead happy, well-adjusted lives.

NO CRITICAL AGE TO TRAIN A DOG

The critical time to begin developing a dog's skills starts when you first get it. I don't care what age he is, what counts is what you do with the dog. I have trained pups and dogs at all ages, and so has my friend Wendell Holeman and many other dog men I know. What's important is sticking to a training plan and staying with a routine of feeding, exercising, and field work.

It does not take a rocket scientist to train a pup. Several people who have gotten pups from me had never trained a dog before in their lives, and have had outstanding success. The reason for their success was good bloodlines, lots of love, dedication in teaching a limited amount of commands, and time spent together at home and in the field. They used no frills, no drills, and no props other than a dog lead, collar, and whistle.

Little pups and little kids just go together.

CHOOSING A NAME

Keep the dog's name simple and positive. The call name doesn't have to be a one-syllable word; it just has to be easy to say. Williams' Pride Shoe was the actual pedigree name of one of my dogs, but his call name was just Shoe. As I mentioned earlier, Shoe was the leftover pup of the litter. No one seemed to want him, but the little ball of white fur would not take his eyes off me. When he was the only pup left, I placed a white shoe alongside him and he would wag his little tail, stretch out, and close both eyes. Side by side, they looked like a pair of tennis shoes. I named him Shoe, and although I had no intention of keeping a pup from the litter, sometimes a youngster chooses you. At night, Shoe slept with the old tennis shoe and during the day, he followed my shoes. Today, I'm running eight of Shoe's offspring.

Shoe always seemed proud of his name. Pick a name for your pup that is associated with something, some-one, or someplace you like. By doing so, you will unconsciously say the name with enthusiasm and affection, and this feeling will be passed on to your pup.

Dogs can learn a lot of words, but their name should be the first one. Make sure the name you choose does not sound like any of your command words. A good rule is to use a unique one- or two-syllable name. Choose a name that is positive, fairly short, and easy to say, and you can't go wrong. Dogs are intelligent animals and a name should communicate trust and respect. Choosing the right name can strengthen a good relationship.

Use the pup's name over and over again, always in a positive way. Get down on your knees to be at the pup's level and call him by name. Open your arms wide in a welcoming posture, smile, and look and act friendly.

Every day before I feed a pup I gather him in my arms, hold him firmly, and repeat his name. Give your dog a hug and pet him as you repeat his name. I don't think it hurts to "jabberwocky" while holding them, as they don't understand the meanings of words and the sounds can be pleasant if spoken softly. I talk to my dogs all the time in pleasant jabberish sounds.

When a pup first responds to his name, praise him so he associates it with something good. Pick the pup up and rub or pat him. A smart pup will learn his name quickly, so use his name every time when calling him to come. Make sure he actually comes when called though. If he doesn't, go get him while still calling his name. Learning his name is important, but *coming consistently when called is the foundation for all good dog behavior.* Keep using his name as often as possible when feeding him, taking him outside, and doing other things he likes.

SLEEPING ARRANGEMENTS

By this time, you will have made sleeping arrangements for your pup. Where he sleeps, be it in your own bed (most people don't want to admit it), in a kennel box next to your bed, or out with the other dogs is up to you. Whatever place you choose should be nearby, at least for the first few days. You are now his whole world, and that little ball of fur needs the assurance that some version of his mother is present.

I have raised pups both in the house and out in the kennels. However, I make sure that my kennel dogs are warm and comfortable. They have long, clean, concrete kennel runs outside that are attached to a building with inside compartments that are warm and free from drafts. Many of my older dogs prefer being outside in their kennels to being in the house.

It's very important that your new pup is as comfortable as possible.

How many times have you heard it said that keeping a dog in the house affects a dog's nose when hunting? Well, I certainly disagree with that. How a dog performs in the field has nothing to do with where it lives. In fact, an important part of my training philosophy is to bring every pup that lives in the kennel into my house for short periods of time. I have found the best time for this is during the pup's daytime sleeping periods. I continue this practice throughout the dog's life. I also periodically take a kennel dog with me in the front seat of my pickup on trips to town. The more time you spend with a dog in the house and around town, the more companionship will develop, and that will translate well in the field.

I have always had kennel dogs and at least two dogs that live in the house. I would surely have more dogs in the house were it not for my wife's differing opinion, although I must add that she is the first to bring a pup or dog in if they are sick. Also, when I'm traveling, she is the one who cares for the dogs I leave behind, and many times she will bring them into the house.

I have kennel dogs and house dogs. Like my house dogs, I make sure my kennel dogs are as comfortable as possible. All of my kennel dogs come in the house from time to time.

Here I am in my office with two Brittanys, Winston and Hershey. The more time you spend with a dog, the more companionship will develop between you, and that will translate well in the field.

At May Pond Plantation, my friend Leigh Perkins has upwards of 30 pointing dogs of different breeds in his kennel. His house dogs are Brittanys and English setters, and their numbers vary from four to seven. Other than one retired setter, the dogs are outstanding bird finders and all ride the mule wagon, taking their turns with the kennel dogs when hunting wild bobwhite quail. When it comes to the dogs' scenting ability, the house dogs do just fine against the kennel dogs.

A look at three of my most recently acquired puppies, two pointers and a small, female Brittany, shows how quickly pups adapt to their new life as long as they are treated with care. Perk, a pointer, was eight weeks old when he arrived. Sally, a Brittany, was seven weeks old when I got her a year later. Pete, the other pointer, was 15 weeks. He arrived a couple of months after Sally, although they are about the same age.

The new pointer pups were kenneled with my old female at different times. She's always been a wonderful mother, and she accepted each pup as her own. I try to get each pup inside for a

My friend, Orvis chairman Leigh Perkins, has a kennel full of dogs. As you can see, his house dogs are also a mix of different pointing breeds.

daily visit right after I feed him because this is usually a rest period, and they readily settle down. When Perk comes into the house, he plays for a short time, tearing newspapers and scattering them around my office floor before going to sleep. Pete settles down at once and takes a long nap at my feet. Each young pup looks forward to coming inside and feels pleased and comfortable in my presence.

Kennel pups adjust readily to living in a home. These two German wirehaired pointers are waiting for a new home.

When Sally arrived she became a permanent house pup. In less than two weeks she was house broken and spoiled a little, but within three weeks she was completely trained to come when called. Later, I moved Sally to the kennels with an older dog. Like all of my dogs, she still gets her turn in the house during the day.

Sometimes a new pup finds its own place to sleep. Sally loves sleeping on my boots I use for cleaning the kennels. I'm sure she scents other dog smells, which helps her feel more secure.

EATING ARRANGEMENTS

My kennel and house dogs are all fed twice a day in the kennel area. My procedure goes like this: Twice a day all the pups and dogs are exercised together under my supervision in a large two-acre enclosure. I clean the kennels, give them fresh water, and prepare their food while the dogs are exercising. There are two dogs to a kennel run and they are fed together, with a dish for each dog. I stay and watch all of the dogs eat.

This procedure is important. All the dogs know they get to exercise and then come in and eat. Calling them to come is easy. They have a routine and look forward to being fed. The young pups learn to come when called during this routine, and it is reinforced for the older dogs as well. If any dog does not come on my command, I go get him and bring him back on a lead. A dog cannot get away because he is in an enclosed area.

Each dog returns to its kennel run, gets a drink, and waits to be fed. This reinforces the dog dominance idea, and my procedure is always the same. I'm with them when they exercise, I make them obey when called on command, and they eat under my supervision. The dogs know I'm the leader of the pack.

New pups are also fed twice a day. At first, I feed a house pup in the house, but after several weeks they go out with the other dogs to get fed. Give your new pup a good brand of dry chow and mix it with hot water. Feeding times are morning and evening. If any food is left over, as it often is with pups, I pick up the dish. The regular feeding place and time informs your pup that you are in charge, and it gets them used to the routine. Don't feed your pup at any other time, even if they are hungry — stick to the same routine.

Should you feed a pup table scraps? I do. If the food is good enough for me it's good enough for my pups and dogs. Leftover meats, fats, and some vegetables, mixed with puppy chow, are nutritious and can stimulate a dog to eat, although I only give them small amounts with their food.

My kennel dogs get as much attention as the house dogs. They exercise early morning and evening before feeding time, even if going afield that day.

If you give a pup too many goodies it may stop eating its chow. If this happens, I refrain from giving it any leftovers until it starts eating its main food again. I do not recommend feeding a dog at the table or in the kitchen when cleaning up or preparing food. (But I will admit that I've done both.) I believe it does not have any detrimental effect on your ability to train a pup. For some reason, many trainers believe that having a dog sleep on the bed, feeding it from the table, or having it in the front seat of a vehicle is contrary to good training methods. It may not establish the behavior pattern that many trainers like, but it doesn't have much to do with how dogs will work birds. Is it spoiling a dog? Call it what you like, but to me you don't spoil a dog by doing these things. Having a dog with you as much as possible is a helpful tool when training because they are more apt to want to please you and respond more favorably to you. Just because you feed them a few table scraps does not mean you have lost control over them. Just don't go overboard.

Do not let your pup get overweight. If this occurs, I cut the amount of chow and stop feeding table scraps. Usually, though, my dogs are working hard and hunting every day, so I pack food into them, feed them supplemental canned meat products, and give them any table scraps I happen to have. (But no bones!)

A HAPPY PUPPY

As mentioned earlier, the first week should be as pleasant as possible for the new pup. The easier you can make it during this time the sooner training can start. It is essential that you and any other family members establish a good rapport with the pup. A happy puppy is a curious pup, and a curious pup is willing to learn.

Eunice Colmore holds one of her red dog pups (Irish setters). You can certainly see much love is involved when she raises a litter of puppies.

At first, only one person will take the place of the mother. That person is the one who feeds the pup. Within a few days, the pup also will form strong ties with other members of the family. When I get a new pup, it not only responds to me but also to my wife. Later, my dogs associate more with me because I become the alpha dog and take them hunting, but that does not mean they forget other favorite people.

You and other members of the family should spend as much time as possible getting acquainted with the pup; the more time spent the better. When the pup becomes confident of his new home and comfortable with the family, I put a collar on him and introduce him to the outdoors to explore under my guidance several times a day.

This first outside adventure may start when the little puppy looks for a place to urinate. He'll show you he needs to go by looking around or running in circles. Try to pick him up in the running stage. If he does go, don't scold him. Just take him outside, but stay with him at all times. Each time I take the pup out, I let him stay a bit longer. Call him by name, reinforcing the command to come.

After a while he'll look to go outdoors himself, and that's when I put a lead on him. Let him fight the lead (he may do this for some time). Talk to him, stayingË persistent but gentle, and after a few minutes he may respond to the lead and start pulling to explore. This resistance to a lead is normal, and after a few more outings he will start to pull you around. Later, he can be taught not to pull when on a lead.

COMPANIONSHIP

When the pup becomes adjusted to his new surrounding — and this does not take long — he'll seek companionship. Dogs are gregarious animals from birth, and need companionship because they are pack-oriented. This interaction between the pup and you is important, but you also have to maintain complete control as the leader of the pack. A pup gains your companionship through the attention and affection you show him. As this companionship grows, a pup's response to it is a willingness to please you, and this creates a foundation for learning.

Eunice Colmore shows Bobbie Williams, Kessly Lovec, and Robin Lovec her new litter of red dogs. Every one of these pups will be good hunters because they come from great hunting parents.

When a pup is kept in the house early in life, even for a short period of time, that companionship is established much faster. This can also be done with a dog that lives outside in a kennel, but it is your responsibility to spend as much time with a kennel pup as you would a dog in the house.

It is essential for a pup to form an attachment to the person (or people) who cares for him. When a pup has an attachment to his owner, his mental and physical attributes are developed and he will respond more readily to learning a command. The pup/person companionship is a vital aspect of a dog's early life.

Take the pup with you on errands whenever possible. Pups that are not exposed to the world become terrified of new surroundings. Take him to the store, to get the mail, or to get gas. At first, these should be short trips with little time spent away from the car. Put the pup in the front seat with his head on your lap. Crack the window and let him look out and smell the air, but don't let the pup stick his head out the window. When you leave the car for a short time, put him in his kennel crate with adequate ventilation and in a tolerable temperature. (Remember that the temperature inside a car can rise quickly.) When the pup is out of the chewing stage, I no longer use a crate. It won't take long for him to become confident, and he will look forward to going with you.

Some pups get very car sick. To overcome this, set the dog next to you or in your lap and take only short trips. As he becomes accustomed to the motion, take him on longer trips.

Take him for a walk in a park, in the woods, along a river, etc. A pup is just like a kid — he likes to go anyplace you go. Sometimes you may need to use a leash

or a check cord when you are close to a road or some other potential hazard. I try to avoid situations that require this, though, as my goal during the first three months is to let the pup run.

These two young English setters are on the way to becoming good bird finders.

I once bought a couple of pups from a breeder and friend. He said he had a nice female that he would send. He also mentioned another female pup out of the same litter that was very shy. He explained that when she was less than a month old, something harmful happened to her and she became very frightened.

Both pups were beautiful, but the small one, as he had warned, was extremely shy. I called her Daisy because she looked like a little flower. She was a cute little two-month-old Brittany when I got her. She came from wonderful bloodlines, and I was determined to make a bird dog out of her. I kept Daisy with her littermate until she became accustomed to her new surroundings, but she still refused to come out and play with the other dogs. Twice a day I would open the gate to Daisy's kennel run. Her littermate and the rest of the dogs would go out and run around in the large exercise area. The kennels are connected to the exercise yard and the whole area is visible from the kennel runs, but I never saw any movement from Daisy.

She always came out and ate at my feet during mealtime. I would pat and sweet-talk her, but when she finished she only wanted her kennel box. For several more days, I continued to open the gate to the kennel run when exercising the other dogs. I'd call her by name, though only once. She would poke her head out of the kennel box, but would go no farther. Each time I would walk away with the other dogs and ignore her.

About two weeks passed before she came out into the kennel run, but again no farther. It seemed that she found the chain-link fence of the kennel run to be

Daisy was my sweet little flower.

protection from the outside world. Still, I ignored her. This went on for two or three more weeks, until one day she ran out and joined the other dogs for a moment before heading back into the kennel. Each day she would come out and stay a little longer. I kept quiet, never saying a word. It seemed like forever, but she finally stayed with the other dogs for the full exercise period.

Several times a week I take the dogs for a short run in my grassland field. It's about 12 acres and the perimeter is fenced in barbed-wire, roughly a half-mile around. The dogs are not allowed to cross the fence, although they are free to explore the whole field. There is a gate between the exercise yard and the big field. When I take the dogs for their run I just open the gate and they come streaming out, going full-tilt into the field.

The next hurdle was getting Daisy out into the big field. It took over four months before she made the full circuit of the perimeter with the other dogs and me.

I often took her for rides in the pickup and as long as she was in the vehicle, Daisy was fine. She loved being with me. After a year, I decided it was time to let her go with the other dogs to look for wild birds. There was no need to take any gun along, as she wasn't ready for a loud noise. She was doing great until we came to a four-strand barbed-wire fence, and she refused to cross it. I ignored her, crossed the fence, and walked parallel on the other side. Daisy did not cross for at least a half-hour. When she did, she seemed to be one happy dog. I believe that was the day she finally broke that invisible barrier.

Her first experience with a shotgun blast didn't phase her one bit. Daisy became very intent on point, and when I walked past her she loved to flush the birds. Daisy and her sister were both excellent bird dogs. My little wildflower and my great male Shoe became an excellent breeding combination, and every pup they produced turned out to be a strong, hard-charging, obedient bird dog.

COMMANDS, ANYONE CAN DO IT

A command is a direct order given by one in authority. The word "command" makes many folks uneasy. We don't like it when someone gives us a command, so why should your new pup? First, a dog's behavior is very different from ours. People, when adults, are free to do as they please as long it conforms to the general rules of our society, but dogs can only think within the framework of a dominance order.

Kessly works on commands with one of my new Brittany pups.

Dogs assume that people also are a part of this order. And this is exactly what you have to do — become the dominant partner in a pup's life. A training command can't be learned until both sides know who is in control. If a dog does not think you are "top dog," then this dominance process breaks down and you will have lost the ability to make him obey. Therefore, teaching a command has to be executed with authority, and in a way that makes the dog respect you. If you are the dominant force in its life, the pup will always want to please you.

When I exercise my dogs, they never run free and are never left unattended. Even my older house dogs are supervised when let outside. When I'm with the whole gang, every dog honors my authority. Sometimes when the pack gets together, the younger dogs display strong body language gestures, but they respect my position as "alpha dog" and stop short of any serious fights.

When a new pup or dog is initiated into my kennel, the introduction is done one on one with each dog, and I'm always present. It does not take the new arrival long to learn its place in the order of dominance. I believe the new pup learns from the others that I'm number one.

My wife, Bobbie, takes care of my dogs when I'm gone. They certainly love her, but she often has to re-establish her authority. Whether they accept her as top dog is still questionable. She occasionally gets tested, and sometimes a dog thinks her command does not have to be carried out.

Anyone can teach a command to a pup if they show that they are in control. This should not be by force, of course, but by making a dog respect you. If rewarding a pup with a treat works for you, that's fine. I use treats when teaching a pup its name, but not very often beyond that. As soon as they understand the

Bobbie Williams praises our young pointer, Pete, after he responds favorably to a command.

command, they learn quickly that pleasing you earns them praise or a reward. Once a pup associates a command with something good, praise becomes just as effective as giving it a treat.

When a pup gets older, I believe praise works even more effectively because the dog respects your authority and dominance. In a hunting situation, praise works to the hunter's advantage because he can provide positive reinforcement each time the pup points or honors another dog.

LEARNING TO GIVE A COMMAND

Learning how to give a command is as important as a pup learning to respond to it. As mentioned earlier, the first command a dog should learn is its name. After that, other basic commands should be taught, and no two dog trainers seem to use the same words. My theory is to keep the commands simple and few. I use commands only for keeping a dog under control and for helping me hunt. I will get into the specific command words I use later, but I believe everyone should find words they are comfortable with because each person communicates differently. Basic commands should be simple, one-syllable words, although when the pup gets older I use two words or combine a word with the sound of a whistle.

This brings us to actually giving a command. First, you have to get the dog's attention by speaking its name. Say it with a voice of authority. The tone or inflection is as important as the command word. Use a pleasant facial expression when calling the dog. Don't call a pup to come like you are asking it to pass the butter at the breakfast table. It's not a request to come; it is a command. Smile when you are pleased and scowl at the pup if it disobeys your command, as dogs pick up on these cues. Just as when teaching kids in school, you cannot talk in a soft monotone. Dogs react better to a low, deep voice, but keep the sound normal. Don't use a high-pitched scream. When calling a pup, face in his direction and make eye contact at all times until he comes to you. Even make eye contact if he is at a dis-

It doesn't take a rocket scientist to train a bird dog, but a lot of love sure helps. Here, Kessly teaches a Brittany pup the command "come."

tance. Body language also encourages the pup to respond to come. Use a low, welcoming position, smile, and talk in an excited tone of voice. If the dog is close to you, the command can be soft, but it still needs to be firm.

If I get no response, I raise my voice. Stand tall and look big; you are the alpha dog. If I have to call him a third or fourth time, I go toward the pup and call to get his attention. Getting the pup's attention and making him come to you is the most important lesson he will ever learn.

Later on, there is nothing wrong with disciplining a pup for wrong behavior. Put your hand out, lower your voice, and say, "No!" sharply. Most pups respond better to a lower tone. To them, a guttural sound is more like a growl, and it means "pay attention right now." After a pup learns to come — I mean absolutely always, all the time — you know you are in control and all future commands will come easy.

WHAT'S IN A COMMAND

The basic commands for training a pup are *come, whoa, stay, stop, sit, OK, heel, no, down,* and so on, but I don't use all of these. With some dogs, though, more command words are necessary. For example, I never use the command "whoa" with some dogs because I don't have to. If a young dog points, holds, and backs like a rock at a very young age, there is no need to teach the word. The command "sit" is another good example. Someone once asked me why I didn't teach my dog Winston to sit. My answer was that Winston hunts; he doesn't have time to sit. When I call him back, it is understood that he circles to check in and returns to hunting. No time

lost. For other dogs, like retrievers or dogs that live in the city, sitting may be very important.

As a puppy grows older, I use other commands when field training, such as *kennel, load up, easy, fetch, hunt dead, dead bird,* and *let's go.* An older dog can learn a lot more words than you might think. I also talk to older dogs a lot when they are feeding, playing, or exercising. They may not know the words, but they sure like the happy sounds I make, and they respond by making happy sounds back to me.

After the pup has learned its name (and that is a command), the next most important command is "come." This command word supersedes all other commands because, once learned, the dog is always under control. It can be used in combination with many other commands, such as "come—sit" or "come—load up." The

Rip, Perk, and Pete, three of my hard-running dogs.

command "come" is also important when starting a pup in the field. This is the key to controlling the pup at home, in town, and when he is running right out of the country.

There are several ways to teach a dog to come; voice, whistle, and hand motion can all be used, either singly or together. An electronic device like a beeping collar system can be a great aid, but I have reservations about using an e-collar (shock collar) on a pup, and even on most older dogs. I only use one sparingly and only as a last resort.

"Come" is the command that means, *I'm the dominant dog, get over here or else. If you don't, I'll come and get you and you'll be in big trouble.* A pup has to learn to obey immediately without thinking. No matter where my dogs are, even when sleeping, they automatically respond to "come." My dogs respond to the command because they want to please me. I am tested sometimes, of course, but I always follow through and correct the problem immediately.

A pup responds best to short, crisp commands, and some commands should be given with obvious hand signals. Saying a command over and over is fine, but slurring words

The command "Come" is the foundation for a dog that hunts for its owner. Voice, whistle, open the hands, get down on one knee, and welcome him to come to you.

together may confuse your dog. Give commands clearly and with inflection in your voice. I always use the dog's name and the command together.

Once the command "come" is learned, I use it with other words, such as "come on." You may be wondering why I do this, and my response is that, besides the dog's name, which is already pleasant to him, other words or sounds will also become pleasant if used in a happy way, as in "Come on, old boy." Say it with love, and a dog picks up that pleasant sound from a companion he also regards as his leader and adopts a happy attitude as a result. Facial expressions and eye contact that accompany the command "come" are also important. Smile and use welcoming body language when he comes, but by all means, make him respond immediately when called.

When outdoors, I use the dog's name and "come" and introduce a high-pitched whistle right after the words. Once the dog learns to come on command to the whistle,

A little affection goes a long way in getting a young dog to come. Cole Claiborn gives his young Brittany a big hug for coming in.

I no longer have to call using my voice. In the field, I also add a dramatic hand signal, putting my hand high in the air and waving. With my training method, I use the whistle and the hand-waving signal only for a dog to return to me and not for anything else.

I use the word "no" when disciplining a pup. This should be said in a firm, sharp, but low tone and be accompanied by stern body language. When a pup disobeys, say "No!" and scowl.

I use "OK" as a release, either from a specific command or in praising good behavior, as in "OK, good dog."

Command words are also used for implementing restrictions, and a pup has to learn to accept this. A pup may not want to comply when he is told to get down or stop an annoying activity, but learning to accept restrictions early in life will carry over to accepting discipline in the field.

Words are just sounds to a pup, so stick to simple ones when giving commands and make sure different command words don't sound alike. As the pup gets older, you can expand his sound vocabulary as much as you like.

TRAINING SESSIONS

Training should be enjoyable for both you and the pup. Pups have a very short attention span, so command lessons should also be short. Sessions lasting five to ten minutes are fine. Before feeding is an optimum time to train because a pup is mentally more alert when hungry. A command word should be repeated the same way each time in order for a pup to learn quickly.

Once a pup obeys the fundamental command words indoors, I repeat the training session outdoors. Only give commands when you know you are in control and can assure compliance. Training is not a substitute for exercise or play time. Training is work for both you and the pup, but each session should begin and end on a happy, positive note.

Ben's Dogs

Pete: A Bit High Spirited

Pete is a handsome black and white pointer whose mother and father are descended from famous bloodlines. Pete joined my Brittanys and the other two pointers when he was four mouths old. His dark brown eyes are surrounded by jet-black fur and sparkle with enthusiasm. His temperament is highly spirited. Even at a young age, he seemed to be driven to run fast and wide. But Pete also has another passion. He loves to retrieve anything close at hand. Small rocks, sticks, and even long branches will be dragged about when he is in a happy, playful mood. He learns quickly and is not jealous or quarrelsome with any of the other dogs.

Though he will never be large for a pointer, Pete gained muscle mass quickly and began to stand out as a strong-running dog at six months. As a puppy, he pointed butterflies that lit on the fence at the end of his run. Unlike the other kennel dogs, Pete spends a great deal of time pacing back and forth in his long run. He is not hyper or hard-headed, just driven to run and run hard. When Pete is in my office for short stays, he settles down quickly underfoot and goes to sleep.

Twice a day before feeding time I run all of the dogs together in their exercise yard, even if they go afield that day. It's a routine I've always followed: old dogs, young dogs, and pups all run, play, and socialize together. This is how I introduce the social structure of pack order in my program.

I use no commands when I open the kennel doors of the runs; the dogs just come pouring out. But when Pete was introduced to kennel life, being very lively, he developed the bad habit of bolting out of the kennel door before it was fully opened. So for him I had to adjust the routine a bit.

Understanding and accepting the differences in individual dogs makes the task of communicating with them much easier. I do not over-train any dog, but with Pete's outstanding, spirited genes, I needed to tailor my approach in helping him become an excellent bird dog by starting him from the get-go to be obedient before he ran. I don't believe most dogs need to be taught to sit and stay on command, but in Pete's case, the command "sit" was my control method for stopping him from bolting out the kennel door. After he sits a while, I release him with the command "Okay." Still, the most important command for Pete, as with all my dogs, is "come." Young Pete is on his way to being a crackerjack bird dog. His hunting skills are in his genes, but obedience has taught him to hunt for me, not for himself.

If needed, I change my method of training a dog. Pete was one of them. The top photo shows how I make him sit before each daily run. First, I let the rest of the dogs out, then I tell Pete he can come out, but I again make him sit just outside the kennel. Finally, I let him run free.

Part Three:
The Classroom

SIMPLICITY BRINGS SUCCESS

All people communicate in a variety of ways throughout our lives. No matter what you do for a living, having good communication skills is important. It's also true when training dogs. A person's personality plays a role in training a dog, so what works for me may not work for you because my communication skills and personality are completely different than yours. What's important is that you develop your own standard for training. After reading this book, take what you believe is important and add it to your own training model.

My college years in secondary education and my long teaching career were beneficial in developing my philosophy of how people learn. Working with adolescents in the classroom and coaching field sports was a learning process, not only for my students but for me too. My goals for students were to create a good atmosphere for

Dez Young with Hank, an English setter. Dez is the producer and host of the television show "Hunting With Hank," who is the star performer in the series.

responsive learning, develop each individual's innate skills, promote respect by working with others, and achieve camaraderie. My philosophy in understanding and working with hunting dogs is quite similar. Both pursuits have been very satisfying.

Dogs are also individuals. Each has its own personality and genetic makeup. Each dog has various instinctive skills and a different learning curve. No two dogs respond to learning in exactly the same way. Observe your new dog carefully as an individua l— different than any other canine you may have had. If a dog is sensitive or frightened of things ("soft"), my approach to training is quite different than with a dog who is bold and aggressive ("hard"). Understanding and accepting these differences has always made my teaching task easier, as it will yours. Never over-train a bird dog; good genes are better than complicated training techniques.

Jim Fergus, author of A Hunter's Road, *stops a moment to praise his French Brittany.*

I treat my dogs as if they are students who just need a little love, tender care, and a chance to learn. Whether I'm training a pup or rehabilitating an older dog, I treat them all the same. Gaining a dog's trust and confidence is essential. Gaining a dog's friendship is paramount. If they act mischievous they get verbally disciplined, but I then show them affection so they understand that while I did not accept that behavior, I still like them.

House dog or kennel dog, after their morning and evening meals they get a biscuit, a hug, some petting, and I address each one using its name, "Perk, good dog." If you express affection towards your pup, he will become trusting and obedient.

When training a dog, work to bring out his good traits. Simplicity is the secret to hunting dog success.

PRESCHOOL

Home school is over. The pup should now be well adjusted to its new home or kennel. You have taken him for rides, to the park, to see friends and other dogs, and for short outdoor trips. He has learned his name, comes when called, knows a few connecting words, such as "good dog," and has taken short walks on a lead.

His exercise periods lasted 10 minutes or so for the first several adventures, but they are now much longer. He has explored farther and farther, yet comes when called or whistled in. If not, he's been corrected on the spot, even if you had to go after him. He likes and trusts you and respects your dominance. You are his pal and he is yours. If all of the above is true, his learning thus far has been successful.

I call the next training period "preschool." Others call it yard training, yard drills, or obedience training. Home schooling, yard drills, field training, and hunting birds should not necessarily be an orderly progression. No part of training is separate, and it is always an ongoing process. The only prerequisite I have before taking a pup or dog into the field is that it must come when called.

While dogs continue to learn throughout their lives, as they get older learning is more innate than controlled. Keep in mind that learning for a dog has two important facets. First, it learns from its owner, the dominant partner or the one in charge. This facet involves learning obedience through commands. This is very important for controlling a dog, but it has nothing to do with his skills in the field.

The second facet is by far the most important. Being a good or excellent bird finder has nothing to do training — it's all in the dog's genes. A pointing dog with excellent bloodlines has the innate ability and solid instincts to point, honor (by backing other dogs), and retrieve. A smart dog learns to hunt birds on his own from his genes, not from a trainer. A good bird dog is 95 percent genes and 5 percent training, and that 95 percent in dogs more than compensates for an owner's lack of training ability.

I feel over-training and using too many training aids can prevent a dog from fully developing its natural instincts. Teaching too many commands, manipulating a young pup to point or retrieve at a young age, or controlling every move it makes during training will do more harm than good. A dog's innate abilities will develop as he grows. For example, I never teach a pup hand signals to quarter or zigzag across a field. A young dog learns on his own, by instinct, where birds are going to be and searches those places.

TOOLS FOR TEACHING

You don't need many tools to train a dog. First, I buy a series of inexpensive collars in graduated sizes so the pup has a collar that fits throughout its growth period. Once the pup is fully-grown, I get a good, sturdy 1-inch collar that has a center ring and a brass name-plate. I have several leads of different lengths and a lone check cord.

Next comes a good whistle. There are a variety of excellent whistles on the market today, but I prefer one that is small, brightly colored, and plastic, with a rich, resonant sound capable of carrying long distances. The brands I use are the Roy Gonia or the Acme Thunderer. A good, braided-leather lanyard for the whistle is a must. I also use the lanyard for carrying other items such as a small comb for burrs and hemostats.

You don't need many tools to train a dog, but adequate hunting and dog supplies are essential when going afield.

Andrea Donner hooks up three pointers to the chain-gang.

I own several different kinds of electronic collars, and I am a firm believer in using beeper collars. A .22 blank pistol for introducing a pup to gunfire is useful, but a supply of small and large plastic bubble wrap works just as well.

I recommend three different methods for staking out dogs when necessary. I attach hooks with rings to the back bumper of my pickup and then use a short chain with solid brass snaps on both ends to hook the ring on the bumper and the center ring of the dog's collar. This allows me to keep the dog under control while I get training gear or hunting equipment out of the truck.

The second method is called the chain-gang, and every dog I own is accustomed to it. This is simply a long chain with stakes at each end that are driven into the ground. A series of short chains come off the

main chain at intervals of about four feet. Dogs are hooked to the short chains, which I call a string.

The third method is a one-dog setup that just involves a single swivel stake-out rod with a short chain. The single stake out and bumper hookup are ideal for a single dog.

All three stake outs are important in my home and field training programs. When a string of dogs is on the chain-gang or staked out, they can watch others being trained or worked. I also use these stake outs to feed or water dogs at rest stops when traveling and to get them out of their kennel compartments in places where I layover or hunt.

Many trainers and dog enthusiasts have a wide array of additional equipment, but my dog training stuff is bare bones — that way I have more room for dog biscuits.

Gary Thomas hooks up his beautiful young Brittanys to the bumper of my pickup truck before getting out his hunting gear.

While working many dogs together in the field, I sometimes use the chain-gang method.

A single stake-out comes in very handy in the field while taking a break or having lunch.

COMING WHEN CALLED

I've stated several times that coming when called is the most important lesson a dog learns. I also want to emphasize that when I say, "Winston, come!" the response is immediate. Follow through every time, and never let a pup ignore the "come" command. This command absolutely has to be carried out. I also integrate whistle and hand movements with the verbal command. The whistle is an important control in the field.

So how do I go about making sure every pup learns to come on command? Here are some methods that can be used.

THE REWARD MODEL

For openers, when you first used the word "come" you strengthened this command by giving the pup a biscuit or showing it affection. You are the pup's substitute mother. You feed and take care of him and are later the dominant force in his life. He is intelligent and eager to please, so the pup responds by coming to you. The process is repeated over and over again, and the pup learns to come immediately. Be firm and fair to the pup so that he wants to please you. This model of teaching a pup to come works wonderfully because dogs are obedient, respond quickly, and train easily. But there are always a few that need additional training. If the pup thinks you are not in control, you no longer have the boss status.

THE DOMINANCE MODEL

It's natural for a pup or young dog to get excited in new surroundings. This is particularly important for hunting dogs, but they also have to learn restraint by responding to your commands. By now the pup has learned to come to you, but that has mostly been because he wanted to. He has not been compelled or forced to come, so he may test you. If the pup does not listen, you have to show him who is the alpha dog.

If a dog does not respond to a blast or two on the whistle, it gets my attention. I call his name with authority, blow the whistle with authority, use my hand movements with authority, and walk toward the pup with authority. When he does come in, I don't praise him. I scold him and say "bad dog." You may disagree with this, but I also pull his ears a bit (although never harshly).

Remember the wolf dominance scenario. The alpha male shows aggression by opening its mouth over the other wolf's head and pushing down on the ears and growling. To the pup, my "bad dog" is just like growling, and when I pull his ears it is the same as the wolf pushing down on the head and ears. Like the wolf, I'm demonstrating my dominance by using light aggression.

Some folks will say that their pup is too sensitive for this treatment or that they don't want to break the dog's spirit to hunt. That's for you to decide, of course, but it's a lot better having a dog hunt for you than on his own — and years of experience have shown that this method is effective without traumatizing the dog.

There is another technique that I use sparingly. It can be a useful tool, depending on the pup's personality — out comes the rope.

CHECK CORD MODEL

I have very few dogs that need this type of discipline. Most of my pups are taught to respond when called with the reward method, but some dogs need a bit more discipline because of their lack of obedience training as a pup.

My dogs are all lead trained, so the pup will already be familiar with a check cord. The check cord is less than 15 feet long with a brass snap at one end. It's a good idea to let a pup drag the lead or a short rope when young, just in case the force model is implemented.

First, put a stake in the ground. With the check cord on your pup, loop the rope around the stake so he is next to it and you are facing him. The stake holds him so that he cannot come to you voluntarily. I then flip the rope to roll it free of the stake. At the same time I call his name, command "come," and blow a whistle.

This series of pictures illustrates putting a check cord around a stake, which holds the pup in place so the trainer can move away without having the dog follow.

I pull the rope toward me to enforce the command, but when he comes on his own I no longer pull the rope. I go down on one knee, open my arms, and praise him for coming, saying "good dog, good dog." I repeat the lesson until he comes in every time on his own. Once he does, I take the check cord off and let him run a short distance before calling him to come. If he does not respond quickly, we start over.

This series shows how to release the check cord around the stake, then call the dog to come. This is a very effective way of teaching a dog at any age to come when called.

THE E–COLLAR MODEL

I use e-collars only on rare occasions and believe they should never be used for training a pup. As far as I'm concerned, they are a last resort for any dog. An e-collar (electronic shock collar) is a device that has two parts: the transmitter, held and controlled by the person, and the collar that goes on the dog. The device is used to reinforce a command by shocking a dog.

When e-collars first came out many folks thought them inhumane, and with good reason. They had one, high stimulus level. Over the years, e-collars have improved immensely. Today, they are state-of-the-art training equipment. Most brands have three or more intensity levels for stimulating (shocking) a dog.

I don't believe that the electronic collar is a tool for teaching commands. It is a device that enforces what a dog has already learned and refuses to obey. In the wrong hands or with an inexperienced trainer, e-collars can still be cruel and detrimental to a dog's training.

Some dogs never make the connection with where the shock is coming from. So it is imperative that a dog understands who is giving the treatment. The e-collar should never be used to torture a dog for doing something wrong. It's a tool that has to be used with extreme caution.

If all other methods fail, and you need to enforce the come command, use the lowest possible level of stimulation while calling or whistling the dog to come. Stop stimulation as soon as the dog responds. The stimulation method is not a substitute for the come command, and it should only be used if the dog doesn't respond to the other methods.

E–COLLAR SOUND MODEL

I have developed my own way for using the new e-collar models. One of my e-devices, and I'm familiar with all the e-collar manufacturers, is made by Innotek. It has multiple functions with different stimulation levels and a beeper system. Innotek's transmitter can turn the beep on the collar on or off. It can also activate the beeper to sound continuously to locate the dog. I have been able to teach several pups and young dogs that the continuous beep is a command to come. This has worked very effectively — without any need to use the stimulation program.

Tritronics has a collar with a recall sound to command a dog to come back, but due to its high frequency only the dog can hear it. At this time, the Tritronics hunting dog models do not have this feature, but I'm sure that the models that do would work in the field to recall a dog.

WHOA IS ME

Many trainers will tell you that "whoa" is the most important command they use when hunting. I would have to disagree, as I believe the command "come" is. If you can't find your dog, you can't give the command "whoa." If a dog refuses to point or back another dog, "whoa" can be a useful command, but it is a command with which you and the pup have no physical contact.

In a situation where a dog is refusing to honor a point, I use the command "come" instead. This gives me complete control over the pup because he is at my side. He can still back, but I'm in full control of him as I walk toward the other dogs. Let me add here that when I first start a pup in the field, I let him go if he steals a point or breaks for the birds. He gains confidence from the experience and will eventually learn on his own.

If using "whoa," teach it to the pup before going to the bird field, as an enthusiastic pup often challenges this command. With all the excitement that a pup experiences in the field, the "whoa" command has to be reinforced continuously.

This is not a difficult command for a pup to learn, and there are many different ways to teach it. One method is to hold the pup on the end of rope around a stake as described in the "check cord method" previously discussed. Give the command "whoa" several times while snugging up the cord around the stake and facing the dog. Then give the command "come" and flip the rope from around the stake. He'll soon learn he has to stand still until you release him.

Another way to teach "whoa" is to simply hold the dog firmly in place on a lead or by the collar while saying "whoa" over and over again before releasing him. Once the dog learns to hold still, call him to come, and then put your hand out and say "whoa." If he does not stop, place him back in the position he was in when you gave the command. Some dogs understand what you want faster than others, but they all will learn through consistent repetition.

It can be confusing for a pup to learn the command "stay" for one situation and "whoa" for another. In

C.D. Clarke, an outstanding artist of wildlife watercolors, moves up behind his liver-and-white Brittany, anticipating a flush of Huns at any moment.

reality, these convey the same message. So I keep it simple by just using "whoa-stay" together as one command. I have found that combination command words are much stronger and more forceful. The combination "whoa-stay" is a lot like saying "Winston, come."

One last thing to remember: the words used are unimportant, it's the consistent way the command is given and enforced that is critical. "Whoa-stay" or "hey, whoa" — there is a difference.

Later, I practice the command "whoa-stay" in the field when hunting. I do this because I believe a pup is at his best and is more alert when hunting than at any other time. Also, they do not want to screw up, and the two-word combinations show dominance and authority.

A WORD ON OTHER COMMANDS

I do not let my dogs jump up on people or put their front paws up on things, so I teach the command "down." This is easily taught. If a pup jumps up, I raise my knee quickly and surprise him and say "Down." But I have many friends that let their dogs jump up, and that is okay, too. Having the dog put his paws on them is a way for both dog and man to show affection. If that works for you, do it.

As far as I'm concerned, the command "down" has little importance when hunting, but if you live in the city, this command and others like it may be necessary because there is a lot more socialization and interaction with humans. *Sit, whoa, easy, heel, down, up, kennel,* and *load up* are all useful in certain situations, but what command words to use is entirely up to the individual.

WHISTLE BLOWERS

A whistle is essential in controlling a bird dog in the field, but it is often misused. As a professional writer and photographer, there are times when I follow other bird hunters with their dogs, and there is nothing more annoying than a person continuously blowing a whistle. I'm sure you've been in similar situations and feel the same way I do. In most instances, the whistle blower gets no response from his dog anyway. When hunting with friends, I make it clear, the less noise the better.

One whistle blower explained to me that the reason he keeps blowing the whistle is that his dog is so intense when working fresh bird scent, she only concentrates on one thing at a time and does not hear it. He has a fine dog, but she sure has him fooled.

Like my pointers, my Brittanys are big running dogs and trained in big open country. With all of my dogs, I teach them to check-in often. When they come in, I wave them on and they go back to hunting. By doing this when they're young, they learn on their own to check in, hunt for me, and not get lost.

My primary purpose when using a whistle is to call the dog to come. I do not use two blasts on the whistle for this and three blasts for that. One of my friends suggested that when hunting with him I use two blasts on the whistle for my dogs and he would use three blasts for his dog. I explained that my dogs know the tone of my whistle and the distinctive way I use it, so it wouldn't be a problem.

When I'm hunting with more than one of my dogs — and that's most of the time — I consistently use the same procedure. The dogs learn who is being called. If I want all the dogs to come, I use more blasts on the whistle and they learn that, too. No matter how many dogs are on the ground, a whistle should still be used sparingly.

Another method I use depends on the situation. If hunting with experienced dogs, I teach them several related commands using the whistle. One is to "check in and be on your way." When the dogs come toward me, I wave them on and they go back to hunting. This method keeps them under control but saves valuable hunting time. If I'm changing direction, I get the dogs' attention by blowing the whistle. As they turn to come in, I use hand signals, pointing and walking in a new direction. They quickly learn that I'm not calling them in, and they adjust to move in the same direction.

Yelling, screaming, jumping up and down, and giving constant hand signals have no place in my training method. These things just confuse the dogs, and they will eventually pay no attention to the useless orders. Another reason for not using unnecessary sounds and motions is that they scare game birds. Many times the birds will flush long before you see them. The fact is, when hunting any wild game, especially late in the hunting season, even a small noise like talking quietly has an impact on birds.

THE WING GAME

Many dog owners and breeders take great pride in showing off their seven-week-old pups pointing a bird wing attached to a string on a long pole. Is this an indication that the pup is going to be an outstanding pointing dog? My observations have shown that it does not matter one iota whether a pup points a wing or not. Mostly, it makes the owner or breeder happy in showing off his pups.

My conclusions are based on the pup's performance in the field. I've had many outstanding pointing dogs that paid no attention to the wing. In other words, whether they sight pointed earlier in life made no difference in my dogs' performance in the field. Don't forget that it is the nose that locks up a dog. Sight pointing involves a completely different sense and has no connection to the nose.

I don't train dogs to play the wing game, but young Winston likes to sight point robins on the lawn. This is not pointing; he's just having fun. Sight pointing has no bearing on how well a dog performs in the field.

This is just fun pointing for a dog. Dogs also have fun pointing other things. I've had dogs point houseflies, robins, blowing leaves, and even the wet mop head I use to clean kennel floors. Last week, my new five-month-old pointer pup, Pete, locked up on point while looking through the plate glass window at dried flower pods moving in the wind.

Years ago, I had a dog named Pepper. His specialty was pointing flying aircraft and their vapor trails, but Pepper was only an average bird finder — even though he did hold his head high. I also had a female by the name of Gina. When I took her fishing with me she would point the rocks that had water rushing and splashing over them.

So for anyone that likes the wing-on-the-string method, I would have to say that I have never found it helpful in picking a pup. My cat even stops and points momentarily before pouncing on a wing. Frankly, I would prefer a pup to pounce on the wing and chase it when it moves, rather than point it.

This training method is nothing more than a game for you and your pet. Some claim it is useful today because a pup is restricted more to

My good friend and hunting partner, Steve Claiborn, knows when Rip points, he's got birds.

the backyard and does not have the chance to get out often to hunt, but what your dog does in the yard while playing with a wing is not going to teach him to point live birds. Pointing is innate and done foremost with the nose. The wing game is not going to move his development along any faster. I think it's irrelevant in helping a dog point.

WHEN TO GUN

It has often been said that no dog is born gun-shy, that it is man-induced. Think about that statement. I would suggest that all animals are actually born sensitive to noise. A loud noise startles any living creature because it's not a frequent occurrence. What happens when you hear a sonic boom or sudden loud thunderclap close by? We all react in some way, and it scares the heck out of some folks.

I certainly don't recommend trying this, but I have been present when a shotgun was fired next to a herd of cattle. They were off in a cloud of dust. Have you ever experienced a gun blast from a hunting partner next to or slightly in back of you? The noise is devastating to your ears. A dog on point or backing in front of the hunter gets the full impact of the blast of a shotgun. As discussed earlier, a dog has acute hearing that is remarkably superior to ours. They are much more sensitive to loud sounds than we are.

When a dog spends many hours in the field, the sight of a gun is associated with something good like hunting birds, although that does not translate into a dog loving the sound of a shotgun blast. It's still an irritation, but the sound means something good is about to happen.

Hershey is a roan-colored Brittany, and a great bird dog.

My dog Hershey is 10 years old. He has had thousands of shots fired over him and he has never been gun-shy. Last year, while making a hunting movie for the Outdoor Life Network, the sound director asked me to shoot 10 to 12 times so that he could record the echo of the blast. It so happened that I had two dogs down on the ground waiting for me to go hunting. After several shots with my 28-gauge side-by-side shotgun — which compared to a 12-gauge is not loud at all — Hershey jumped into the front seat of the pickup. The director assumed that Hershey was trying to get to our lunches, but I explained that he wanted to get away from the sound of the gun. Hunting dogs put up with loud noises, but they don't like them any more than we do.

There is always much discussion on the subject of how to introduce a dog to the gun. Some will tell you that shooting a cap gun during mealtime or playtime is a good way to introduce a dog to the loud sound of a gun. After the pup accepts that noise, you move on to a louder 22-caliber blank gun and then on to a shotgun.

Others recommend starting this same procedure with a pup in the field. Both methods work, but many times a pup is much too young for a gun lesson. What these two methods have in common is that the sound occurs while a pup is doing something routine like running, playing, or eating.

A loud noise is not a learning situation; it's just an irritation that a dog has to overcome. Timing is critical when introducing a loud sound to a pup. Remember, no matter what the pup's age, it has to be done with extreme caution. When done correctly, it takes gradual and repeated conditioning to make it work.

Miss Kessly is checking if her new pup is uneasy around a popping noise. At first, start far from the pup when popping the bubble wrap. Then move closer if the pup is not irritated by the sound.

No matter what method is used in curtailing gun-shyness, it's important to be aware of the pup's reaction. If there is any indication of uneasiness, the lesson has to be stopped immediately. If the lesson is continued and the pup has a negative reaction, it's too late. You have done more harm than good.

My method of building confidence while noise training is carried out in the field. The key is to introduce the loud sound when something good happens after, not during, the irritation — bird in the air, pup in motion, dog concentrating on flushing quarry. The sound is distracting, but it is now part of a good experience.

My method can be used with wild or liberated game birds, but a young dog has to have many hours of field experience with birds before I fire a gun around him. Learning to hunt, exercising, finding birds, and noise irritation are all carried out together, and these each occur during the same outing, which also saves time.

Private lands, public lands, hunting preserves, or bird dog hunting clubs are excellent places to train confidence building in a pup. Let the pup get some hunting hours under its collar and get it into birds, whether they are pen raised or wild. When the birds are pointed and flushed, let the pup run, but shoot only once. He will concentrate on the birds flushing instead of the sound. You can use a cap gun or a .22 blank pistol, but I just use bubble wrap. If the pup accepts this sound, a louder one may be tried.

If the pup reacts to the noise and comes back to you, praise him, saying "good dog, good dog" often. Afterwards, if the pup walks with you, ignore him and keep walking, but don't shout or force him to get out from underfoot. Sooner or later he will gain confidence and be on his way again. Do not shoot again that day. Make sure he has found several more birds before shooting again.

Bubble wrap is a great training aid, and it makes a good pop. It can be concealed so the pup can't associate the noise with an object as well. Most folks have only one dog, and with bubble wrap there is no need to buy an expensive starter pistol.

Common sense dictates that you not have a young pup around any fireworks or shooting at field trials. Never have him present when shooting for fun or around shooting ranges and gun clubs.

RETRIEVING, NO FORCE PLEASE

Every dog is a natural retriever with innate ability handed down through countless generations, but that does not always relate to a pup retrieving birds to hand. Some dogs are reluctant to retrieve or will bring a bird halfway back and drop it. Some choke on the feathers and refuse to retrieve at all.

Before frustration gets the better of you and drastic measures are taken out on the dog, analyze why the pup is doing what he is doing. It could be an issue of dominance or aggression, but most times it is just inexperience. Force training in this situation may be more detrimental than helpful. Many dogs just need time to sort it out on their own.

When hunting pointing dogs on wild birds, on a scale of one to ten (ten being the most important), pointing, holding a point, backing other dogs, relocating and backing again, and finding downed birds all would get tens in my book. Retrieving a wild bird to hand is not that important. It would only be a four.

Eddie Gonzales'
German shorthaired
pointer brings in a
plump sharp-tailed
grouse. This short-
hair is a natural
retriever with
innate ability.

That may come as a surprise to some hunters. In fact, I believe locating a downed bird is the most important part of retrieving. I teach every dog to hunt dead. When a bird goes down I prefer a dog to be on it as soon as possible, and this means that they are not steady to wing and shot.

Teaching a pup to hunt dead is a simple task. Go to where the bird dropped — never assume it is dead — and walk around looking down while repeating "hunt dead, hunt dead" over and over again. The pup should know a bird is down or that you are looking for something. He will quickly understand your enthusiasm and start looking by using his nose. Later, many of my dogs will hunt dead even if no bird is shot. They know by my words and actions that I'm looking for something, and they want to be part of it.

Once the interest in finding birds is achieved, dogs connect picking up a bird and retrieving it with your enthusiasm, and they are more inclined to bring it to you. When a dog is looking for a dead bird, you are looking also. If you are close by, go down on one knee just as soon as the bird is found and encourage him to bring it to you. By being close at hand, you assert yourself as the dominant force, and he will fetch the bird to you with little time to think about what is going on.

When a new pup finds his first bird, let him smell it and pick it up. It's okay if he drops it. This is new to him, so let him be alone for a short while and do his own thing. No two dogs react the same. One pup may

John Nash, an outstanding dog breeder of English setters and an excellent train-er, works diligently getting his dogs to retrieve to hand. It may come as a surprise to some, but I believe it's more important for a dog to locate a downed bird than bring it all the way to hand. . . but to each his own.

pick up the dead bird and run away from you. That's a good sign — at least he picked it up. He is probably too excited to think about retrieving. Some pups will bring a bird only part of the way, and that is okay too. Others will stand over the bird. Just let them work it out. This is an important lesson a pup has to learn on his own. Most pups, as they mature and gain more experience, will come around to retrieving without any force training.

Let's take a pup that only retrieved halfway as an example. First, I'll happily meet any dog halfway because retrieving is not a pointing dog's main job. Finding birds and pointing them is. His next most important job is finding downed birds; retrieving comes in last. I have also found that if I pay less attention to a young dog's inability to retrieve to hand, he will usually begin on his own.

Yelling, getting upset, or running after a young dog is the worst thing you can do. Play it cool, and you'll be surprised at how a dog will finally start to retrieve. It's all in the genes.

If a pup or a dog brings you the bird and will not let go, understand that he has brought it to you because of your dominance, despite the fact that he wants to keep it, too. So what happens? Lockjaw sets in. Pull down on the loose skin under his hip where it connects to the belly and he'll let go.

C.D. Clarke takes a rest on the steps of an old homestead after hunting sharp-tailed grouse and Huns with his Brittany.

Force training to retrieve is not in my program. If it's not going to be natural, I'll live without it. I don't believe force training is in the best interest of pointing dogs because many times you can break their spirit, and then the pup or dog will not want to hunt dead.

TAKING A DOG INTO THE FIELD

Folks have often asked me at what age a pup should start field training. My advice is always the sooner the better as long as he comes when called, although this does not mean that an older dog that hasn't had field work is at a disadvantage. If a dog is started later, say at 12 months of age, and has good instinctive hunting genes, he will be able to learn more quickly than a youngster. So it is easily possible that a year-old dog could surpass a pup that has had more field experience. If a dog is birdy and has desire, he can catch up in short order. I've received several year-old dogs that had no field training or experience whatsoever, and they became outstanding gun dogs.

Age has little to do with a dog's intelligence, although intelligence has a lot to do with good performance in the field. Instinctive hunting genes are important, but time in the field is the element that brings out the best in a smart bird dog— no matter when they are started.

Dave Meisner, the founder of Pointing Dog Journal, *prepares to go afield. Gilly, a hard-running pointer, waits for the command to go.*

Ben's Dogs

Clyde: Sometimes His Character Gets in the Way

Clyde is named after Clyde Park, Montana, which was originally Madame Bulldog's stage stop. When the post office was established the new town was named Clyde Park. ("Clyde" because Clydesdale horses were present on several ranches, and "Park" because the valley has a park-like appearance.)

Well, the name fits Clyde well. He is built like a bulldog and runs like a horse, but he would be just as happy lying around greeting folks getting off a stagecoach. Clyde's a good bird dog, but he will never be a great one because his character gets in the way.

Clyde is a character, but sure fun to hunt with too.

He has never been top dog in the field, although he does sometimes make the "A" team. He is a dependable hunter most of the time, but occasionally he fools around when he should be hunting.

Clyde likes to travel. He even spent a short hunting season with a friend in northern Mongolia. When he returns home, he fits in with the other dogs as if he never left, but Clyde is a loner when hunting. When I put several dogs down with him, he goes off and does his own thing, although he still finds his share of birds.

Clyde is a laid-back dog, easy to train, responds well to commands, and will hunt with anyone. He's a good bird dog — most of the time. You see, for Clyde, hunting birds sometimes gets in the way of other activities. Clyde's greatest fault is that he loves to pursue bunny rabbits. He knows that when he starts to give chase I will call him back, and he comes readily. But Clyde has his own plan, and for several seasons he fooled me. This is his routine: He always comes back when called, but he also remembers where the bunny went. So when he starts hunting again, he runs far off to one side of me and pretends that he is hunting birds. Then, when I'm not looking, he doubles back and looks for the rabbit. He's usually successful in finding it and has fun with the chase. When I finally realize he is missing, I blow the whistle and he comes back panting and out of breath. He doesn't think I know, but since Clyde is such a character and is getting older these days, I let him have a little fun.

If your dog chases a bunny for sport now and then and you call him and he comes back, nothing has been lost in that day's hunt. Hunting should be fun, not only for you, but for your dog. Clyde would certainly agree.

Perk: Leave Him Be, He Wants to Please

Perk has always wanted to please, but some dogs are just that way. For a person who knows little about training a bird dog, Perk would be a dream dog. Perk is not a run-of-the-mill pointer. He's a big-boned, handsome male, mostly white with lemon-colored ears. He looks like a prizefighter, but he is strong, quick, and seems to float when he runs.

Perk has everything going for him: speed, range, style, bird sense, and an outstanding nose. But his best quality is that he handles as comfortably as an old worn glove and has since he was a puppy. He always comes when called, and I never have to use a command more than once for him to respond.

At nine months he was a strapping model of a pointer, two-thirds dog and one-third pup, but he didn't have a clue what the other dogs where doing when they locked up on point. He would just stop and look at me, probably thinking I had something to do with it. He was unsure of himself and did not want to

Perk has speed, range, and is a bird finder. When he points or backs, he's all business.

foul up. I would walk over to him and talk softly, encouraging him to go toward the other dogs, even if he flushed the birds. This same drill lasted for over a month with no change, and I began to have doubts about whether he would ever back the other dogs or find birds on his own. I'm not a trainer who gives up on any dog that comes from good bloodlines, though, and I figured time was still on his side.

Conditions where perfect early one Sunday morning. The first dew of August clung to the golden grass, and the temperature was around fifty, with a light wind moving across the rolling landscape. Scenting conditions appeared to be better than they had been for the past month.

While driving to the training grounds, I went over the crest of a low hill and saw a large covey of young Huns cross the two-rut road. I stopped about a quarter of a mile beyond where I saw them and put Perk down. I wanted to give him a chance to find the covey on his own.

Things don't always work out as planned, but sometimes they work out better. Perk galloped swiftly into the open field. He turned and looked for me, so I called him back to change his direction. He raced along the rutted road and passed where I had seen the birds. In that instant, turning in his stride, he slammed into a high-tailed point and never moved a muscle.

Perk grew up that morning. Today, he's all dog and no pup. And when he isn't the first dog to find birds, he backs rock solid. Perk has all the instincts of his craft, and since that day he has used them well.

Part Four: Prep School

PEN–RAISED BIRDS

I have no qualms about working a new pup on pen-raised birds. If executed properly, the introduction of planted birds can be a helpful training tool for a young pup, although working pen-raised birds is not going to make a bird dog an accomplished, all-around hunting companion for every kind of bird hunting.

Planted birds have certainly changed the way most dogs are trained, and in some areas, they have revolutionized training methods. It may be the only way for an owner to expose his young pup to birds if he lives far from wild bird country. Training and hunting on preserves or pay-as-you-go shooting clubs is a good way to start a pup on the road to becoming a bird-hunting partner.

The lead Brittany points a rooster pheasant in a choke cherry patch just over a hill. Lewis backs but can not smell the bird.

There are various methods of training with planted birds. I believe the best one is to release the birds randomly in a field. Liberated quail, chukars, or pheasants all work well because they have a tendency to move around after being released, and they lay down a lot of scent.

A dog first has to learn to scent the birds, and then find them on his own. By doing this, the pup also learns to work the cover and actually hunt. If a pup does not point at this stage and flushes the liberated birds, that's fine. You should try to only use birds that are strong fliers, though. If he has good genes, it is only a matter of time before your pup starts to point, especially if he has a good nose.

One has to be careful not to work a pup on liberated birds in the same location over and over again. Too much exposure to planted birds in the same area will have an effect on the pup's desire to explore on his own. It doesn't take long for a young pointing dog to figure out planted birds. This repetition becomes more of a drill than a hunting experience.

Having your own scent on pen-raised birds can't really be avoided. Nor will human scent dissipate quickly after a planted bird is placed in the field. A dog with a good nose has an uncanny ability to keep track of its owner by backtracking the man's scent trail. I have seen this demonstrated many times in the field. When a dog becomes lost, it will even backtrack its own scent. Human scent stays in the field a long time, and a dog can track a person's activities long after that person is gone. A bloodhound is able to track a particular man's scent for days, and a fur trapper de-scents his traps, clothing, and even his footprints to avoid leaving human scent. When in the field, my dogs can smell or sense the whereabouts of water — as do other animals — and they remember these locations from year to year. Man has no way of understanding how complex a dog's smelling system is; he can only assume its magnitude through observation.

My point is that dogs have the ability to smell everything in their environment and then sort out whatever

it is they want to key in on. So once a dog learns that you are planting birds, he can make the connection and track your scent to find the birds rather than hunt for them. You need to be very careful that this doesn't happen.

For the person who has only one or two dogs, I don't recommend trying to raise game birds or keeping a quail pen or call box. It's not worth the time involved for what your dog accomplishes from it. The time taken in rearing and caring for game birds is better spent running your dog. Also, once your dog has worked a number of liberated birds, no more are necessary. Going to a preserve over and over may be helpful for some things, but it is not necessary if you have access to wild bird country.

I do not keep pen-raised birds on my property, but if

Perk found the birds first, but because of his low tail is unsure of their true location. Rip and the two Brittanys are also pointing and not backing. This indicates the birds are moving.

you decide to, just make sure they are kept a good distance from the dog's living quarters. Years ago, a friend of mine kept a few quail. When I would stop there my old bird dog would go to the quail pen, wag his tail, and then come back to me. He was an experienced bird dog and no longer pointed birds in the yard, but with wild game he never broke point until the last bird flushed.

If planted birds are held stationary with restraints or release traps, the process quickly becomes too mechanical for the pup. This is also true during many field trials. The dogs know in advance the fields in which birds are planted. As I suggested before, liberated birds should be randomly released, and even the hunter should not know the exact location. This will go a lot further in simulating a wild bird experience.

Pen-raised birds can often become a little like the wing game. I call it "plant a bird, bring up the pup." It becomes only a superficial pointing experience whose real usefulness is in reinforcing a pup's pointing ability and in keeping a pup steady to wing and shot — not in helping a dog learn to hunt.

It works something like this: A restrained bird is put down (whether it is hobbled, shackled, or held in a release trap is unimportant). The trainer knows where the bird is, but the pup doesn't. At this point, there is more human scent laid down than bird scent. The pup is carried or led close to the bird. Hopefully, the pup picks up the bird's scent, often just a foot or an inch from his nose. If he doesn't scent the bird, that's okay. He is just held with the lead. If he points, the lead is held so he cannot move. The bird is flushed and the gun fired. The pup bolts and is held fast by the rope, and he learns not to break after the flush. Lesson accomplished. Or was it? What did the pup actually learn? If he scented the bird and pointed, fine. If he did not point, he is held by the rope and waits for something to happen. He sees the bird being flushed and isn't allowed to move. This is an introduction to becoming steady to wing and shot, but in my view, a pup doesn't learn anything about finding birds or hunting.

We have no idea when any pup is going to connect its nose to its brain and point, so why force him to hold? A bird dog's nose is its brain, and a pup may start pointing at three months or a year and a half. It's innate; he either has it or he doesn't. There is no need to push a pup too early or force it into artificial situations. When a pup's nose fills with bird scent, it triggers something in his brain and the light just clicks on to point.

I assume that in getting a new pup your goal is to have a good hunting dog, but many folks have limit-

The pose of this pointer is a good indicator that the quail are close by.

ed time to train one. So for the amateur trainer, working a young dog on liberated birds can be rewarding and may save time. But don't get the wrong impression from this training. This liberated bird work is useful in a dog's first few training sessions, but after too much of the same thing, the dog is no longer learning. He is just repeating what he has already learned. If a pup has a good nose and starts to point, he will continue doing it for the rest of his life, without this repetition on planted birds.

A pup learns to hunt and handle birds by exploring new places where wild birds live. Now it's time to expand your bird dog's hunting experience and head out for new horizons.

WILD BIRDS

After hunting liberated birds, most people eventually want to hunt wild birds, but many of these same folks believe wild places to hunt no longer exist. This is certainly true in many parts of the country, but there are still plenty of places to hunt wild birds. The truth is, there is more good wild bird hunting available today than at any time in the past 50 years. One only has to look. The rest of this book is devoted to hunting wild birds. For your dog's sake and yours, it's time to move on.

Upland bird hunting is as American as baseball and apple pie. In some families, the hunting tradition has been handed down from generation to generation — and so has the prized family shotgun. We've all heard the testimonials: "My grandfather passed this Parker 12-gauge side-by-side shotgun on to dad and he passed it on to me, and someday it will be my son's or daughter's gun." But what most of these families weren't able

Darren Brown is about to walk past Winston into a bunch of sage grouse.

to pass along is a place to hunt. So in today's world, many traditional, family-oriented hunters believe hunting wild birds is no longer a possibility.

This may be true around many of the population centers east of the Mississippi, but head up to the northern woods or cross the big river and hundreds of miles of wild bird country still exist. In fact, much of the North American continent still has some type of upland bird hunting available. More than 20 species come under the category of upland game bird and may be taken during an open hunting season, and every one can be hunted on public lands.

The popularity of upland bird hunting in the past 20 years has been growing by leaps and bounds. Spending time hunting with your dog, a friend, or your children is still a great American tradition, and miles and miles of private, state, and federal lands are still available. One just has to load up that new pup or seasoned hunting companion and head out.

SELF–TRAINING

My theory of letting a dog train itself on wild birds goes back to bloodlines. I always look to excellent genes that carry the natural ability to point, back, and retrieve. The bloodlines also need to show intelligence, which expedites self-training. A smart pup develops quickly and learns to hunt cover that holds birds. Desire to hunt also aids in self-training, but for a dog to self-train, you are going to have to get him in the field as often as possible.

Let's assume the dog has gotten through the home school and preschool lessons fairly well. You have worked him on a few liberated birds, and he is raring to go. But the first time you are together in a wild bird field, your whole concept of what to expect of your dog has to change. In effect, you are starting the whole bird-finding process over from scratch. The only part you have played so far is to teach your pup a few commands and, hopefully, to find a place that has wild birds. Now you are dependent on the dog to find the birds. It's all up to him.

I don't know which Brittany found the birds first, but they got 'em.

Or maybe the pup has gone through home school and preschool and started running on his own, but has not been worked on planted birds and has not found any game birds yet. The difference between these dogs is that the first one is more than likely a bit older, with a few more hours of bird experience. This older pup may be farther along in the learning process, but he is not any more advanced in finding wild birds.

The second pup, which we will assume is not as old, has had the opportunity to run free and is already comfortable working new cover. This pup is just being a pup and exploring the world around him.

For all practical field-training purposes, my method of working both of these pups on wild birds would be the same. If a dog has been hunted on liberated birds for several seasons, it certainly will be more advanced and will adjust faster than a dog just starting out. No matter what age they are started, though, every dog that is introduced to wild birds has to go through the same self-training process, and every dog, no matter what the breed, learns at a different rate. Even though some pointing breeds mature earlier than others, this individual learning rate is innate.

This pointer has the birds pinned down. You can see it in his eyes.

When scenting conditions are ideal, one dog may pick up scent several hundred yards away, another dog at thirty feet, and yet another dog may scent much closer, although the last dog may later develop a very cautious, masterly approach when picking up bird scent. As a trainer, there isn't much you can do to improve a dog's scenting ability; it is just something they are born with.

In the early 1950s, I purchased two female Brittany pups from the same litter. One was liver and white and the other orange and white. Gina, the orange and white Brittany, could wind bird scent at a great distance and pointed birds farther away than most dogs. Lola, the liver and white dog, had a much weaker scenting ability. She rarely picked up bird scent before her sister. The truth is, when Lola pointed, there was no mistake because she would be eyeball-to-eyeball or right in the shadow of the bird's tail. To this day, I'm still prejudiced against liver and white Brittanys, although I've certainly seen some very good ones.

In self-training, a dog's nose is in harmony with the environment and tuned into finding wild birds. A dog's self-training involves smelling the flowers, chasing tweety birds, false pointing old scent, overrunning its nose, and flushing game birds. And, oh yes, pup is going to chase furry critters like rabbits or deer, but the *come* command learned in preschool should correct that desire in short order. Remember, a pup should always have fun in the field. Let the dog be a dog.

As a dog learns to hunt on its own by being exposed to wild birds, that knowledge is retained and carried on from season to season. A dog also learns different techniques when hunting different species of wild birds. After a couple of seasons, your dog will have matured and gained a variety of valuable hunting experiences, so conditioning is all that will be needed from one year to the next.

A savvy dog never forgets how to hunt wild birds because that scenting ability is locked in the brain. An experienced dog knows more about finding birds than the hunter, but the hunter also has to learn how to read bird habits and learn bird habitat. Good cover is what holds wild birds, and the hunter has to put his companion in birdy places. The dog will do the rest.

SELF–POINTING

As I mentioned earlier, you don't need to have seasoned dogs in the field to train a pup. If a pup has what it takes, he will learn the ropes himself. The only advantage a pup gains from working with older dogs in the field is that he will follow the other dogs and cover more ground, which accelerates the desire to hunt. A pup on its own is a little more reluctant to cover ground when it first starts, but that changes quickly with more time in the field.

I'm a firm believer in natural field training and in letting the dog use its natural ability to hunt. I once asked my friend Thomas McGuane what his secret was in training cutting horses. His reply went something like this: "Ben, I can only train a smart horse because it's already in him what to do." It's the same with bird dogs. I don't train them; I just give them the opportunity to learn.

A first-year pup will break on birds or chase them, but he soon learns that he can't catch them and starts to train himself not to do this anymore. These are learning sessions for a young dog. A self-taught dog will point and learn to hold until the bird flushes. We don't give enough credit to the dog for what he learns on his own.

My Brittany, Hershey, is the best all-around bird finder I have today. He made his first point on a wild rooster pheasant. I had been working dogs on young sharptails in a Conservation Reserve Program (CRP) field when Hershey seemed more interested in being alone than being with the other dogs. I heard Hershey's beeper collar broadcasting in the pointing mode off to my left, but I figured he had just stopped to smell something. I paid little attention to him until an older dog honored his point. This got my attention, and I hurried past the trailing dog and walked up to Hershey. He didn't move. In the barrow pit next to the dirt road the dried grass was only inches high. I looked up and down the lane and saw nothing. Hershey still didn't move. I walked down the slope, and a big rooster burst from underfoot.

This is Hershey's tenth year, and he has never pushed a point in his entire life. He never breaks until the last bird flushes, and he honors every dog that points. He learned all of this from working wild birds, starting with that rooster many years ago.

A pup chasing birds after the flush is completely different from a dog moving or breaking on point before a flush. If you want a pup to be steady to wing and shot, chasing birds has to be curtailed, but it has absolutely nothing to do with stopping a pup from moving after it points.

One reason a dog moves from a point is that it has lost the scent of the bird and becomes impatient. Or the scenting conditions may be so poor that he has overrun his nose and before he can stop, the bird flushes.

The pup is not screwing up in this situation, as most dogs will correct this movement on their own as they mature. There are always a few dogs that creep or break when pointing, of course, and this has to be corrected right from the get-go.

This is where the five percent of training that you may have to contribute to help a pup hold steady on point comes in. It's very important that you are sure the pup is ready for the necessary correction. Again, every pup's learning curve is different, and this creeping or breaking could simply be immaturity that will work itself out.

If you are sure the pup has a problem holding point and he will not hold with a simple verbal command, it may be because your command for the pup to stay or whoa was not firm enough during earlier training sessions. Or it could be that the pup is headstrong or just too intent on getting at the birds. Sometimes teaching a pup to hold point is easier with the help of an assistant. Put a check cord on him and let him run. When

Rip, with muscles of steel, moves in slow motion scenting the running Huns. When the birds stop, he stops and then holds his tail high.

the pup points, get to him as quickly as you can and step on the rope. Work toward the dog while keeping the rope tight. Sweet-talk him and pet him, but hold him firmly. Then have the assistant walk in front of the dog and flush the bird. If you can't find the bird, let the pup go. It's okay if he flushes a bird, as you've achieved your goal of having the pup hold for a while.

Most of the time I do this training by myself, and it works just as well. Once you have the pup held firmly, slowly relax the rope and move forward while talking to him, saying "whoa," "stay," or "eeezy." Then hold him again. If this is done two or three times, so much the better. If you can't find or flush the birds, just let the pup go. If he flushes the birds, let the pup run and chase the birds a short distance, then call him back. I think chasing birds a short distance at this point in training is perfectly fine.

All three Brittanys lockup tight, pointing several sharptails in heavy cover.

STEADY TO WING AND SHOT — OR NOT

Back when I helped Walter Oberlin train Brittanys for Oberlin Kennels, we were involved in field trials and many of the dogs were trained to be steady to wing and shot. The same dogs were also trained to hunt wild pheasants and were allowed to break wing and shot. With a little patience, it was never difficult for the dogs to adjust to either approach.

A year after I moved west, I purchased McGillicuddy from Oberlin Kennels, and he became the foundation of the male side of my bloodlines. McGillie made his first point at six months and his first retrieve on the opening day of hunting season. The following spring I entered him in an AKC derby stake field trial as a two-year-old.

In late February of that year, I had located several coveys of gray partridge in a large stubble field. It took

Jeremy Petrie levels down on a large covey of Gambel's quail.

McGillicuddy two, one-hour training sessions to change from breaking after the shot to become steady to wing and shot, and by the fourth session he was completely steady. But within a week after the trial, I made sure he was back to his old routine.

Training a dog to remain steady to wing and shot is essential when running a dog in field trials, but it has no place in hunting most wild upland birds. After a dog points, you may still have no idea where the birds are, as the actual behavior of wild birds often differs from what the hunter expects. If a bird holds tight, so should the dog. Simply walk by the dog and flush the bird. If the bird has moved, though, let the dog relocate too. It knows where the bird went, you don't.

Let me explain. I don't want a dog to lock up and never move. In good scenting conditions, my dogs may point birds from two hundred yards away. A smart dog knows exactly where the birds are on the ground. Even on a quail plantation, bobwhites will often run, and the dogs will lose the birds if they are not allowed to move. Most game birds walk or run when pointed; it may be only a short distance or it may be a hundred yards. Whatever happens, my dogs learn on their own when the birds have stopped and where they've stopped. I don't interfere just to make them hold a nice looking point that is useless as soon as the birds move. I also know when the birds have stopped because I can read it in my dogs' eyes and in

Rick Ruoff walks slowly following four pointing dogs working a large covey of running scaled quail. Notice he is letting the dogs work the birds and he is not running.

their body movements. I want dogs that lock down hard until I get there. Then, as I walk by the dog, they also move and point in slow motion just ahead of me. When the birds stop, the dogs will freeze. That's when I know we've got 'em.

Working wild birds brings out the true hunting instincts of a pointing dog. My method of letting a dog teach itself instinctive pointing — while not being steady to wing and shot — enables a dog to successfully hunt every upland game bird in North America. A good dog will use this instinctive approach to learn to read different game birds in a variety of habitats.

SELF–BACKING

Having your dog back or honor another dog's point is important if you hunt with more than one dog or with other hunters and their dogs. Most bird dogs have a natural inclination to back that will quickly show itself, especially if a pup is run with a seasoned dog. If a dog points, it can learn to honor. Pointing and honoring really go hand and hand, but they originate from two different senses. Pointing is done mostly by scent (although some dogs learn to sight point) and is more instinctive than honoring, which is done by sight. The best way to help a dog develop its instinct to back is to expose it to other dogs on point. The more exposure the better.

A dog that usually hunts alone will quickly learn to self-back when given the opportunity to hunt with other pointing dogs. Some dogs almost never have the chance to hunt with another dog, so don't expect them to honor right away. Dogs that have hunted alone for years may never back another dog. But remember that dogs that do not hunt often with

If a dog points, it will learn to honor and back given the chance.

other dogs have already established a dominance order with their masters, and it's important for them to please their owners. Jealousy plays an important part in a dog wanting to please.

If you are hunting with someone and this happens, you can try several different things: separate and hunt different areas, take turns hunting each dog, or just let your hunting partner's dog steal your dog's point. When I hunt my dogs with other dogs that do not back and steal points, I don't get uptight about it. Hunting with dogs is supposed to be fun, not a competition, and there is no need for a confrontation.

As you can tell from reading this book, I have lots of dogs, and every one of them will back. That's not to say that one or two of my dogs won't steal a point. It's fine with me if they move a short distance beyond the lead dog, as long as they don't flush the birds. Most of my dogs that do creep are actually older and more experienced. Pups and younger dogs are more apt to hang back because they are unsure of where the birds are on the ground. Older dogs learn exactly where the birds are, even if they are moving. They learn to relo-

When hunting upland game birds, seeing five dogs on point makes the heart beat a little faster.

cate their points accordingly, which often makes it look like they are stealing a point when they are actually skillfully working moving birds.

I have an experienced dog by the name of Clyde who challenges his peers for the number-two position when backing a point, although this is not out of dominance. I'm sure of this because Clyde is the least dominant dog in my kennels. It is just where he likes to be.

Do I discipline my dogs when they do steal a point? Yes, but only after the birds have flushed. I call the dog over and verbally scold him, and he knows exactly why he is being disciplined.

Don't discipline a dog that has not hunted with others for stealing a point. Give them time and they will work it out themselves.

In a hunting situation, yelling to discipline a dog for not backing or for creeping can scare the birds. If a dog breaks on me and does not back, I let him go the first time. On the next point, I call the dog over and put a lead on him, walking toward the point while softly sweet-talking him, "eeezy, eeezy, eeezy."

They soon understand what I am telling them. It's in my voice. They listen, react, and stop, watching the lead dog point.

TRAINING MYTHS

Once the mature dog has developed his natural pointing, backing, and retrieving skills, conditioning should still be ongoing. At this point, he has had a couple of good hunting seasons on wild birds, and in your eyes, he is a veteran hunter with few faults. He's your hunting buddy and a good companion.

Somewhere along the line you have probably heard that a completely trained dog should not be worked or hunted with an untrained or undisciplined dog. Smart, experienced dogs do not develop bad habits from other dogs because the skills they've learned with their owners overshadow undesirable acts. Dogs do not like to face the disapproval of their leader. For example, if a friend's dog chases a rabbit, my dogs won't join the chase (although I'm sure they'd love to) because I have control over them, and they have been trained not to chase.

But let's say that one of my younger dogs does help in the pursuit and goes running off. This can be a good learning experience for him because I now have the opportunity to discipline the dog and teach him not to chase rabbits anymore.

It is also quite common to hear or read that you should never shoot an unpointed bird for fear that your dog will stop pointing birds solidly. Or that you should always try to shoot birds if your dog does point so that it is rewarded for pointing. I have never found either of these two situations to be confusing for a dog, and they do not cause a dog to forget its training. If a person trains his own dog, it is doubtful that the pup would forget its training, but if a person buys a trained dog or has his dog trained by another, well, that's different. I've seen a lot of well-trained dogs become untrained in a hurry because the new owner had little authority over the animal, lacked a good rapport, and had no understanding of what to expect from the dog. In other words, there was no camaraderie between the two.

THE MAKING OF A POOR BIRD DOG

There are two ways to end up with a poor bird dog. The obvious one is to buy a dog that lacks good bloodlines. This one can't be fixed, no matter how good the trainer is. The other way comes about when a person does not spend the time and effort necessary to develop companionship with his new pup. This is the person who has no command over his dog whatsoever. This pup grows up knowing he can behave as he wishes, leaving the dog completely out of control. If you've been in the field enough around other dogs, I'm sure you have seen this situation.

No one likes a dog that self-hunts — one who runs out of sight and never listens to its owner. This may still be a good dog that locks up on point and never moves, but this will also be a dog that spends more time hunting on its own, never checking in and getting lost a great deal of the time.

The self-hunting dog is usually owned by the whistle-happy hunter who spends most of his days afield yelling, whistling, or zapping the dog with a shock collar. This is the hunter who follows his dog, instead of the dog working under his direction. This kind of situation can make hunting your dog with other dogs difficult, so pick your hunting partners with care. He or she may be your best friend, but that may not make them your best hunting companion.

Keep a pup in close when you first start her in the field. Each time you call, make sure she comes. If not, put a lead on her and make her come when called. After a lesson or two, you will be amazed how well she responds with no lead on.

HUNTING WITH OTHERS

I don't hunt alone as much as I used to, even though I'm still in the field for much of the year. Hunting alone has several advantages. First, I can hunt more dogs at one time. When alone, I'll put six to ten dogs on the ground at once. There is no prettier sight than a long string of dogs locked up on point. Second, if my dogs screw up, I don't have to apologize to anyone. Third, when one of my dogs points, I don't have to kill birds to have a great day in the field. There are many days when I'm less interested in shooting than in watching the dogs work different habitats. I often enjoy just being part of the overall landscape. I'm certainly not antisocial, but there are times when being alone can help you better commune with nature.

Hunting bobwhite quail at Ichauway Plantation in southern Georgia.

Guy Bonaveer, Leigh Perkins, and Rick Ruoff enjoy hunting their dogs together. When one hunts with friends, who shoots the birds hardly matters.

While I enjoy time alone with the dogs, for years now I've had the opportunity to share my experiences with many outstanding hunting colleagues and new friends. When one hunts with others who share a similar outlook on hunting, it hardly matters who gets the shooting or kills the birds. Being in the field with a friend or two and having several dogs on the ground is truly a path that should be taken more often. For decades, hunting has been my way of spending time with great bird dogs and meeting true friends. I've been lucky enough to have many outstanding hunting friends, but a good hunting partner is still a person to cherish.

As an outdoor writer and photographer, I travel and hunt in many different places with many different people, and having just one hunting partner is not feasible. So I have some suggestions that I feel should be followed when hunting with others. My etiquette requirements may be a little different than yours because I hunt with so many people, but I highly recommend that hunting partners establish some kind of code of ethics.

My own code covers three distinct categories: people, dogs, and quarry.

People: Respect and follow all game laws. Respect landowner restrictions and "no trespassing" signs. Practice gun safety at all times. Always be aware of your hunting partner's whereabouts. Use blaze orange or red caps and other brightly-colored clothing when hunting in high or heavy cover. Respect your partner's hunting space when shooting or walking. Do not be critical of anyone's shooting. Share in all work and chores before, during, and after the hunt. Respect your partner's public or private hunting places, and never return to a partner's hunting ground without his or her permission.

Jim Harrison, author of Legends of the Fall, *is a superb writer, fine bird hunter, and a gourmet cook.*

Dogs: I have owned a wide variety of bird dogs, and over the years I have hunted my dogs with many other pointing breeds — and even some that don't point. I must say that having the number of dogs I do doesn't lend itself to hunting with other dogs. For one thing, it deprives some of my dogs of valuable hunting time. Also, my dogs prefer to hunt with their own kennel-mates. In the field, I give few commands, and the distraction of two people giving instructions can be confusing and may impair the dogs' performance.

Of course, having just one dog is quite different. Many hunting partners who each own just one dog work their dogs together, and it can be very rewarding if the dogs are compatible. If the two dogs are incompatible, both parties need to be observant. If one dog hampers the other's performance, appropriate action should be taken. There is no room for competition between two dogs (or two hunters) during a hunting situation, nor should you ever criticize your partner's dog. If one dog regularly outperforms the other, sometimes the only cure is for them to be hunted separately. Something else to remember: A hunting session is not the time to work out the discrepancies between two dogs.

Never give commands to your partner's dog. If you are hunting with someone and his dog's performance is poor — or even downright terrible — don't be critical.

Dave Meisner, founder of Pointing Dog Journal, *and Steve Smith, editor of* PDJ, *examine a fine sharp-tailed grouse that Gilly pointed and retrieved.*

I'm sure they are aware of it, and compliments are much more satisfying than complaints. Bird hunting should always be fun for you and your dog.

Quarry: Having respect for the bird you hunt is an important part of a good code of ethics. Hunting late in the day can be harmful to most covey birds because they need to reassemble before dark. You should never overshoot a covey of birds when hunting. Searching for downed birds always takes priority over killing more game. Field dressing birds properly is paramount for fine eating, and wanton waste is disgraceful in any type of hunting.

TRACKING YOUR DOG

A beeper or bell is often an important part of a hunting dog's wardrobe. With a beeper collar, you can really let the dog go. They are a great way to keep track of a dog, whether it is in the open plains, agricultural holdings, desert scrublands, or dense forests. When running several dogs with beeper collars, I feel comfortable knowing the whereabouts of every single one of them. Beepers are the first electronic gear for dogs that I've ever used regularly, and I would not be without them.

Beeper collars are not a training device, but are used for locating a dog. In big open country, they are a must. Lovett's Electronic beeper collar is my favorite. For my kind of hunting, they are world class.

Bells are a great aid when hunting in heavily wooded country.

Beeper collars are not training devices, though. They are strictly used for locating a dog, although I've recently started to use them to train a dog to come on command. There are many combination models that incorporate stimulation levels with a beeper system. Others just have a beeper system, which I prefer.

The sound of a beeper collar can also contribute to holding birds tight. I especially like using Lovett's electronic hawk scream when a dog goes on point. I'm convinced that the sound of the hawk scream keeps birds from flushing wild.

Most beeper collars can be controlled from the transmitter with an on and off switch. Later in the hunting season, when birds become wary, I run the beepers in the silent mode, using them only for locating a dog. When a beeper on one of my dogs goes into the pointing mode, the other dogs recognize it and back the sound. Beepers are the open prairie's answer to the bells dogs have worn in the eastern woods for decades, and they are a great aid for far-ranging dogs in hilly country.

Using a bell for locating pointing dogs when hunting ruffed grouse and woodcock in heavily-wooded areas has been a long-standing tradition in North America. There are a wide selection of dog bells available. Many are still handmade, with no two sounding alike. There is even a low-tone bell for the bird hunter who has lost a little hearing. Bells, like beepers, take the worry out of locating a dog on point.

Various bells and beeper systems can be purchased from any of the dog supply catalogs.

Ben's Dogs

Tilly: She Had Class

Chantilly was a great female and produced good pups. For a Brittany, she was a bit long and lean, but she was a dog of action, with outstanding balance and endurance. She paced herself remarkably well and never seemed to tire. Like many other Brittanys I've had, she was all business when it came to pointing and retrieving. I can safely say that she was as good as any female I've ever had.

I had promised a friend a pup early in the year so that he could have a young dog for the next hunting season, but, of course, how many pups a bitch is going to have is not easily predicted. Tilly came up short and my promise of a pup was broken. To set things straight, I assured my friend that he could have the pick of the next litter, but that did not solve his problem of having a dog for the coming hunting season.

At that time I had fourteen dogs, not what I consider a surplus for the amount of time I hunt, but a promise is a promise and should always be kept, so reluctantly I loaned him Tilly until he got his pup.

Well, to be expected, his family loved Tilly and asked if they could keep her a while longer. I agreed, and I never had the heart to ask for her back. She stayed with them the rest of her long life. She had a wonderful home, lots of love, and plenty of hunting time. What more can one hope for a good bird dog?

With Tilly, it was all class when she pointed.

Pepper: He Worked Out His Own Problem

Are dogs like people, or are people like dogs? Pepper seemed to think people were more like dogs. He had an indomitable spirit, firmness of character, courage, boldness, bravery — all the elements of true grit. But he also had a fetish for pointing things, like hawks sitting on telegraph poles, low-flying aircraft, and any other moving object that seemed foreign to him. As a young dog, most of his pointing was done by sight, and the fact was, when it came to pointing by scent, he was only an average bird finder.

Pepper worked out his problem, and became a very good bird dog.

Maybe sight pointing was his way of compensating for having a weak nose. Or it could have been that he was unsure of himself and simply pointed everything that moved. But this dog had true grit; he ran hard, retrieved, backed, and did everything right, except that he spent too much time pointing objects other than birds.

The wing game was Pepper's favorite thing, and I put a stop to that nonsense in short order. Sight pointing is fine — that's what a dog does when backing or honoring another dog's point. And many experienced dogs will sight point birds that are visible on the ground. Whether sight pointing is a learned behavior or innate, it is still a useful tool for hunting, but in Pepper's case, too much of a good thing was not helpful in finding birds.

Every time he sight pointed, I encouraged him to move. I'm not sure whether this helped or not, but as he matured, he became more confident and started finding more birds on his own and spent less time sight pointing. The bottom line is that I believe he worked it out for himself as he gained experience and maturity.

I think sometimes we overreact with too much training and don't give a young dog enough time to work out its own problems.

Part Five: Graduate School

ENJOYING THE RESULT

When you and your dog are comfortable working together to hunt birds it's time to hit the open road, where there's still plenty of good hunting across the country. Twenty gallinaceous species of game bird are distributed throughout North America, and one or more species occupies almost every type of natural habitat.

Human population growth has had a large impact on the traditional range of some game birds, but the Conservation Reserve Program and other cooperative

Both hunters relax after a great day of hunting Huns and sharptails.

efforts have benefited wildlife in many areas. Progress is also being made toward multiple-use on our public lands. State and federal agencies and private industries are providing more support for the upland bird hunter.

The brief description of North American game birds that follows is intended to give you an idea of what is available for you and your bird dog. For a more in-depth study of each species of game bird, see my books *American Wingshooting, Hunting the Quails of North America*, and *Western Wings*.

Pheasants

Originally imported from China over a century ago, the ring-necked pheasant is now America's most popular upland game bird. The introduction of the pheasant to North America was one of the real success stories of wildlife management and a huge boon for the upland hunter. Most of the pheasant's range lies in the northern half of the United States. This wily bird lives in diversified agricultural, riparian, and grassland habitat.

The methods of hunting the wild pheasant are as numerous as pheasant hunters, but no matter which way it's done, the hunter needs a good dog. One way I hunt pheasants with my

Pheasants are the most popular upland game bird in America.

pointing dogs is to work through a riparian corridor. Many of these areas have a meandering creek with oxbows or turns that provide a cut-off place for a dog to lock down solid on a big rooster.

Later in the fall, pheasants congregate in large numbers, and isolated cattail patches and small weedy draws are places where birds will hold tight for a pointing dog. Drive and block hunting is also more effective later in the season.

Running pheasants can give pointing dogs a hard time, but good dogs adjust to work them carefully. Dogs are also indispensable for hunting dead on downed birds.

Bobwhite Quail

For generations of American hunters, the bobwhite quail has topped the list of favorite game birds for pointing dogs. Quail are covey birds and seldom venture far from where they were born. They hold well for a pointing dog and flush with a flurry of feathers. When your dog points a clump of grass, get ready, as these little birds may surprise you.

Today, much of the bobwhite hunting in the eastern United States takes place in the southern, coastal states on plantations managed exclusively for quail. Some have wild birds, and some use liberated birds. In the South, the air is crisp during quail season, and the big aromatic pines glisten in the sunlight. Much of the bird's habitat is heavy undergrowth in "piney"

Bobwhite Quail

forests. Pointing dogs, double guns, and bobwhite quail will always go together.

Tallgrass and mixed prairie once covered the Midwest. Settlers moved westward to plow the land, and the bobwhite quail followed, expanding their range. The habits and habitat of these bobwhites differ from those of their eastern cousins, but it is still the same fine game bird. In the Midwest, the bobwhite is at home where the crops and open prairie merge with riparian forests along waterways and brushy draws. Let your pointing dog hunt the osage orange, caragana, and green ash hedges and windbreaks. These are good bobwhite hiding places.

Ruffed Grouse

Ruffed grouse are regarded as "the king of game birds" by the men who hunt them in North America's boreal forests. Woodland bird hunters often have secret coverts shared only by a few close friends. They are

Ruffed Grouse

silent hunters, listening for their pointing dog's bell to stop. Double guns, light loads, and pointing dogs are an integral part of the northern grouse camps.

Ruffed grouse country anywhere is special, but the northwoods can hold the bird hunter spellbound with a rainbow of autumn colors. Abandoned apple orchards and overgrown fields, worked long ago by homesteaders, are perfect ruffed grouse hangouts. They are birds of forest succession — forests kept young by nature or through human intervention. Logging the mature forest opens the canopy for the growth of understory, allowing grouse to move in.

Woodcock

The ruffed grouse hunter is generally a woodcock hunter as well, and he uses his pointing dog for hunting both birds. Woodcock country is often much the same as ruffed grouse habitat, but woodcock prefer areas of lowlands or wetlands surrounded by shrubs and young forests. Their main diet is earthworms, which they find by probing moist soil with their long bills. Areas along streams, ponds, and seeps, and thick patches of high brush with little ground cover, are their favorite hangouts.

Woodcock

Woodcock migrate from the northern forests to the southern states at a rate determined by prevailing temperatures and winds. There can be great concentrations of birds in an area one day and none the next. Faithful woodcock hunters become masters at knowing the migration patterns and identifying likely holding areas.

Woodcock will often hold extremely tight for pointing dogs, allowing for some great dog work.

Chukar

Chasing chukars is different than hunting other game birds from the moment you leave the hunting rig. Chukar country looks desolate. The chukar thrives in high, dry country full of sagebrush, greasewood, and cheatgrass. Steep canyon walls, talus slopes, rocky outcroppings, cliffs, bluffs, and barren, windswept ridges are all areas they call home.

The chukar is a tough bird and hunting them is for the young, or at least the young at heart. It can be the most strenuous and exhausting bird hunting in America, with long, hard days of uphill walking. Pointing dogs are a necessity in chukar country, as dogs save the hunter a lot of shoe leather over the course of a day.

Chukars are sociable birds, and when a big covey is located and scattered, hunting becomes a lot easier. Small groups of birds lie

Chuckar

extremely well for a pointing dog. Chukars are very vocal when broken up. They start calling soon after being separated, so be patient after you flush a covey. Stop, wait, and listen for several minutes before moving on. Chukars are fast on the wing and depend on the rugged terrain to escape. They tend to run uphill and fly down, making life hard on hunters.

Gray Partridge (Huns)

Gray partridge is their proper name, but they are known throughout North America as Hungarian partridge or just Huns. Years of agricultural development in the steppes of North America created new habitat and increased the bird's range. These birds benefit greatly from agriculture, feeding heavily on cereal grains.

Gray Partridge

For generations, gray partridge have lived in two types of habitat. The classic Hun terrain consists of fields of wheat stubble cut by creek bottoms and clumps of thickets, or bench-land grainfields with brushy draws and hills dotted with sagebrush. But like their ancestors, gray partridge are also birds of the temperate grassland ecosystem. Coveys may not be as numerous on the grasslands as they are around grainfields, but they are there. Much of the prairie grassland topography inhabited by gray partridge is comprised of gently rolling hills, coulees, draws, bare knolls, and shallow depressions that run through an open landscape.

If you only hunt Huns around agricultural land you are missing some great opportunities. Huns are like big prairie quail, and they are a blast for pointing dogs.

Sharp-tailed Grouse

The sharp-tailed grouse still occupies a huge area of North America, living in open country and prairie brushlands. Sharptails utilize a wide variety of foods. Their cruising range is large compared to many other upland game birds because their diet changes throughout the season.

Sharptails demand the best from a good pointing dog. A dog trained on birds that hold tight, such as bobwhites or pen-raised birds, will not do well on sharptails right out of the dog crate. There are several important reasons why sharptails give inexperience dogs a hard time. A single sharptail does not lay down a lot of scent. If the bird is in heavy cover, little scent is given off or the scent that is present is overwhelmed by other odors from vegetation. If cover is sparse, sharptails — like other wild game birds — won't sit still. Instead, they move slowly away from any intruder. Dogs have to be cautious not to push the birds.

Shart-tailed Grouse

If small flocks of sharptails are not pressured, hunting may be good for the entire season. In some areas, though, they form large groups later in the season, and these birds can be very difficult to approach.

Ryan Petrie congratulates Rip for a fine sharptail retrieve.

Prairie Chickens

Prairie Chickens

The prairie chicken was once one of the most plentiful upland game birds in North America, and they were found in most of the open country of the tallgrass prairie and mixed prairie habitat. Today, these fine birds of the grasslands are only found in a few places. The best hunting remains in South Dakota, Nebraska, and Kansas.

Prairie chickens need larger areas of unbroken prairie with non-over-grazed native grasses and weeds than their prairie cousin, the sharptail. They prefer the wide-open spaces provided by treeless, rolling plains. They are best hunted early in the season. Later on, the birds often form large groups that are difficult to approach.

No other bird has lent a greater charm to the grasslands than the prairie chicken. A flock of these birds flushing out of the open prairie just ahead of a pointing dog's nose will thrill any hunter.

Sage Grouse

Sage grouse once inhabited a large part of the western United States and the Canadian provinces. They are our largest grouse, and I think of them as a trophy bird. Thousands of acres of shrub grasslands have been broken up and interspersed with agricultural land over the last hundred years. Unlike most other upland game birds, sage grouse are totally dependent on a single type of plant community and have suffered from this loss of habitat. Sage grouse populations are still relatively secure in several states, and state and federal wildlife agencies are working hard to restore habitat suitable for the birds in areas where their numbers have decreased dramatically.

The country the sage grouse lives in — like the bird itself — is big and handsome. The sight of 20 large, black and white prairie bombers catapulting into the sky is breathtaking. Sage grouse are special birds, and it's a pleasure to hunt them with pointing dogs.

Sage Grouse

Blue Grouse

Blues are the second largest grouse in North America. This is the only upland game bird that moves from a lower elevation to a higher elevation in fall and winter as it seeks dense conifer forests. Nesting occurs in grassland communities close to the edges and lower open parks of the montane forest, so hunting blues early in the season is quite different from hunting them later on.

Blue Grouse

Young birds feeding in the open meadows are quite tame and will let a dog approach or point them within shooting range. Blue grouse generally hold extremely well for pointing dogs, but when flushed, blues — like other forest grouse — will often fly toward some type of thick cover and are out of sight in seconds.

Later in the season, hunting blue grouse becomes more strenuous because the hunter has to climb steeper mountain country in order to find them. Birds become more concentrated later in the year, and it may take a lot of hiking to find them.

Spruce Grouse

Spruce grouse can be found in the boreal coniferous forests across the northern tier of North America. The range of the spruce grouse is enormous, and there are still many miles of woods and high mountain forests that see few hunters. Nearly every good stand of boreal forest in North America has a population of spruce grouse.

Hunt along logging roads, mountain trails, and openings around the edges of the forest. As with other woodland grouse, a hunting dog is very important. While you walk the trails and paths, the dog works the heavy cover.

The bird often feels secure enough to remain on the ground when pointed. When a bird is flushed, it invariably goes to heavy cover, and if missed will usu-

Spruce Grouse

ally fly into a nearby evergreen tree. Getting the grouse out of the tree can be a real challenge and makes for a very difficult shot "on the wing." Birds always seem to put a tree between themselves and the gunner. If a hunter is lucky enough to get a shot and put a bird on the ground, a dog is invaluable in finding the downed grouse in such dense cover.

Gambel's Quail

The Gambel's quail is the most important upland game bird in the southwestern United States. This bird lives in a harsh but beautiful country full of mesquite, cholla, yucca, cactus, and other plants unfriendly to those who trespass. Mesquite-lined rivers, creeks, and sand washes are good Gambel's quail hangouts.

When you find a large flock of desert quail, work them slowly and they will scatter. When the birds break up, experienced hunters know they are in for some great shooting. This is when the desert quail behaves much like his distant cousin, the bobwhite, and holds tight for your pointer. The Gambel's quail is a fast little target and can give any upland bird hunter some challenging shooting.

Gambel's Quail

A hunter has to have confidence in his pointing dog when hunting any new species of game bird. Most pointers adapt quite well to desert quail, but the biggest disadvantage for the dog in desert country is poor scenting conditions during much of the hunting season. Give your dog plenty of water, as water stimulates a sensitive nose and helps the dog pick up fresh scent.

Scaled Quail

The scaled quail is another handsome game bird that inhabits the Southwest. When many hunters think of hunting this area, they visualize sandy arroyos, mesquite, and cactus, and it may come as a surprise to discover that grasslands also exist here.

Hunting scaled quail differs from hunting Gambel's quail. Maybe it's because the bird lives in a more open landscape and their cruising range is larger. They avoid dense thickets, tall brush, and tree-lined washes. Scaled quail are not particularly fond of steep slopes and rugged terrain either. They prefer sparse, open cover, and they are notorious runners, preferring not to fly to escape their enemies.

Scaled Quail

Large groups usually have to be broken up before there is close shooting. Dogs certainly help in scattering running birds. Once the covey is scattered, singles and small groups of birds hold extremely well.

While scaled quail can be difficult for some pointing dogs, I believe it's just a matter of the dog adjusting to a new species of game bird. Scalie country is big, and dogs need to cover lots of ground to find a covey. It is also possible to see dogs at a great distance, so trust your dog and let him go.

Mearns' Quail

The home range of the Mearns' quail is beautiful. It lives in an area of rolling hills, high mountains, deep canyons, steep slopes, and rocky ravines. Most Mearns' quail hunting is done between 4,500 and 7,000 feet. The most important element within the Mearns' quail habitat is an adequate understory, comprised mainly of bunchgrasses and forbs rather than an overhead canopy of oaks.

Some hunters prefer a close-working pointing dog for hunting Mearns' quail. Their goal is to cover a small area thoroughly before moving on. In heavy grass, Mearns' quail lie tight and the scent does not permeate the air, so the birds can be passed over easily. However,

Mearns' Quail

as with hunting any game bird, the selection of a close-working or wide-running dog is a personal choice. Any pointing dog is better than none. A covey of Mearns' quail explodes when flushed and usually scatters. They are fast fliers. A good dog with a keen nose that likes to work singles is ideal, and the same goes for locating downed birds. The Mearns' quail has all the sporting attributes of its cousin the bobwhite quail, and like the bobwhite, it's a bird for pointing dogs.

Doug Tate, an outdoor writer and shotgun authority, enjoys his first Mearns' quail of the day.

Valley Quail

The valley quail, also called the California quail, was originally a native of California and Nevada. It has been successfully introduced in other areas and has expanded its range to many western states.

Valley quail are birds of brushy cover. Their preferred habitat is weedy areas around grasslands and mixed farmland, such as fallow fields, hedgerows, and hard-

Valley Quail

wood thickets. Dense escape cover along riparian waterways and abandoned homesteads is also crucial valley quail habitat.

A bird dog is indispensable for hunting this bird, even though some inexperienced pointing dogs may have difficulty handling a large covey of running birds. Once flushed, singles and small bunches hold tight and a pointing dog is essential. Singles are almost impossible to find without a dog once a covey is broken up.

Of all the game birds native to the far western United States, none is more enjoyable than the valley quail.

Mountain Quail

The mountain quail lives in the coastal mountain ranges of the Northwest. They are the largest quail in North America, and their home is in the mixed evergreen forests, woodland chaparral, and along the edges of mountain meadows. This beautiful quail is associated with dense, brushy cover, and they particularly like areas that have been either timbered or burned off. They shift to lower elevations in winter, following the snow line to feed.

The mountain quail is reluctant to fly, and good mountain quail cover can be hard to walk through. A pointing dog is a great advantage for the hunter when working in dense cover. Mountain quail are interesting to hunt, especially with a good dog.

Ptarmigan

There are three kinds of ptarmigan found in North America. Alaska and northern Canada have hundreds of untouched miles to hunt. Sometimes the three species are found in the same areas, but in most cases, they are at different elevations. The willow ptarmigan is the most abundant, occupying a broad range of treeless country.

Willow ptarmigan have three color changes — fall, winter, and spring — and it is possible to shoot all of the color phases due to the long hunting season.

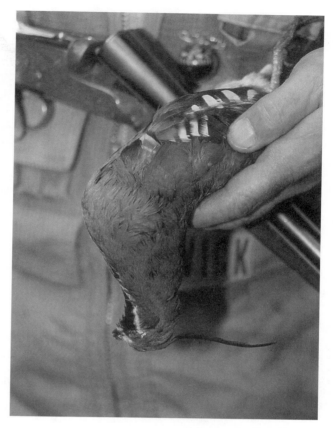

Mountain Quail

The ptarmigan is a great bird for pointing dogs. I'm convinced that either ptarmigan leave a stronger scent than other grouse or the tundra has so much moisture that the scenting conditions are always favorable. Ptarmigan are one of the easiest birds for a dog to pin down, but the dog will also have to learn to sight point.

A large flock can be difficult to hunt because they become more nomadic and move erratically from place to place. I believe this is more from restlessness than a fear of being approached.

Ptarmigan

Hunting ptarmigan with Shoe, a Brittany, in Alaska.

HUNTING TIPS AND OBSERVATIONS

My life seems to revolve around bird dogs and bird seasons, and no matter where I start, it seems I end up in the same places year after year. From August 1 to May 15, the bird hunting season is open somewhere in America, and if you hunt on preserves you can shoot even longer. The first state to open and the last to close is Alaska. Seasons start around early September and close by mid-February in the rest of the country. During the few remaining months, I train and exercise my kennel full of pointing dogs.

Alex Burks and his English setter talk things over.

I'm always analyzing the best way to use dogs to hunt a certain species of game bird. Birds, dogs, man, cover, terrain, weather conditions, time of year, and time of day are all ingredients in a successful hunting recipe. But like any recipe, the right proportion of each ingredient has to be in the mix.

Good dogs are indispensable for successful bird hunting, but this does not mean the hunter will automatically find birds. Recognizing good hunting country and knowing each bird's habits is the hunter's responsibility, regardless of how good his dog may be. Training a pointing dog on wild birds, reading bird movements, and observing the cover are important factors in helping your dog find birds each season. There is plenty of information available to help the hunter gain knowledge of each game bird.

Rick Ruoff assures his sweet little English setter they are going grouse hunting.

All of the elements that make up a good day afield are closely tied together, and each one influences the rest at a particular time. How the dog and hunter approach the field and the birds is also part of the equation.

For years, I have spent a great deal of time observing not only my dogs but other hunters and their dogs who hunt game birds. Many pointing dog owners are amateur handlers who love just watching their dogs hunt in the field. Others are serious, dedicated bird hunters who enjoy shooting birds over a good pointing dog. A few are fanatical dog handlers who expect their dogs to perform perfectly on wild game birds. For the average hunter, the more time spent hunting wild birds, the better the dog's performance will be. I believe more mistakes are made by hunters in the field than by bird dogs.

A hunter can learn a great deal by actually helping his dog instead of just watching him. For instance, it's obvious that selecting a good bird field helps the dog find birds, but I have found there are other ways to be helpful, too.

A problem I have when hunting with guests is that they often don't understand my dogs' abilities, and some have little knowledge of what a good pointer can do. I tell my guests that no matter how far away the dogs point, there are three important things to remember: Always walk toward the dogs on point, don't run; don't talk loudly to one another; and don't yell or whistle to discipline a dog. Reading the individual dog and how it works is the owner's responsibility, and it is as important as reading the cover. Only the dog's owner should give the dog commands in the field.

These three actions have an effect on the birds as well as the dogs. Here's why: If you run and/or start shouting, the dogs may become confused by the

Game birds depend on good cover and camouflage to hide. Where there is good cover, the birds will hold tight.

Andrea Donner approaches the dogs slowly, the way it should be done.

different pace or cadence, and wild birds simply won't hold. Any wild animal that you run toward will run or fly away from you. Game birds depend on their camouflage to hide, then their legs to walk or run, then their wings to fly from imminent danger. This is the birds' protection from ground predators, such as coyotes or man — sight, fright, flight.

It's not often that you see birds on the ground, but they can always see you. Game birds do not feel threatened by dogs, nor are they afraid of ground predators as long as the animal keeps a certain distance and does not run toward them. Unlike men, four-footed animals are part of a bird's normal surroundings. That's why pointing dogs can hold birds. I have found that in running, you lose more ground to birds flushing wild than if you had simply walked up slowly. By walking, the chances are better that the birds will be in gun range when they flush. Your footing is also better, and you won't be out of breath when you shoot. Hunters who run to points often claim the birds may not hold long enough if they don't get to the dog quickly. If the birds are that flighty, however, they certainly will not hold if you run toward them.

One of the best excuses I've heard for running toward a dog on point came from an enthusiastic young man while the two of us were hunting prairie chickens. We were hunting with his professionally-trained pointer. Each time the dog pointed — and it locked up as solidly as stone — the young man would take off at high speed toward the dog, and the birds would flush wild. I explained to him that running scared the chickens. With such a good dog, why not walk? His answer was that he wanted the dog to be perfect, and by running he felt the dog had less chance of flushing the birds. I told him to just have faith in his dog. Today, after hunting several years behind his pointer, I believe he has a good bit more confidence in the dog.

One last thought about running to a point is that you may be able to get away with hoofing it a little faster in the beginning of the season when the birds are young, but as the hunting season progresses and the birds mature, the chances of spooking them becomes much greater.

After getting to the dogs on point, I walk up in back of the dogs. I don't stop next to the dogs or slow down; I walk past them in the direction they are pointing. I know the old saw about shooting over the top of a charging dog, but to me that doesn't hold water. Birds fly in all directions and it doesn't matter where you are, a dog can still get in the way. Just be aware of what is happening in each direction.
My theory is to approach from behind the dogs and into the wind if at all possible. During daylight hours, most game birds are milling around feeding or just moving. Rarely will a whole covey or flock of

birds be stationary at one time. Even game birds that don't form coveys often feed and live in clusters. Some are always in motion, looking out for one another.

My dogs will start working birds from a distance of several hundred yards if scenting conditions are favorable, and they will usually point while still a great distance from the birds. I don't teach this to them; they learn it on their own at a young age. As I move alongside the dogs, they move ahead, pointing again. This can go on for 5 to 10 relocations. I can always tell when the dogs are approaching birds by reading their eyes. I trust the dogs because they know where the birds are.

Dogs worked on pen-raised birds are going to have to make some adjustments when hunting wild birds. Most released birds sit still when a dog points them,

Tom Petrie moves cautiously, not sure if the three dogs have pinned the Huns or if the lead dog has them.

A mother and son spend a day in the field hunting together.

but not wild birds. You cannot expect to find wild birds right in front of the dog's nose because as you walk in, the birds are also likely to move, and they may move in any direction.

You can have your dog hold point and walk in and kick all the clumps of grass you like, but finding the birds yourself can become difficult and may leave you in a difficult position for a shot. Instead, when you walk past a dog on point over wild birds, let the pointer relocate and find the birds again. My dogs relocate automatically when I walk past them. If the birds are nearby, the pointers move only a few feet and stop. If the birds have moved farther away, the dogs will do the same and point again.

Try to think like a bird. When a dog points, what is the most likely move the birds will make? This is why learning a game bird's habits and observing where a covey, a flock, or a single bird flushes after being pointed is essential.

When Rip's tail and head are held high, you know he has birds.

I believe the single most important reason for walking up in back of the pointers when hunting any wild bird is that the dogs and the hunters occupy the same space or corridor. The birds feel less threatened when intruders are coming in from only one direction.

There are hunters who think that after a dog points, it's just a matter of going in and shooting. The way I figure it, that's wrong in any hunting situation. A smart hunter observes and analyzes several things before walking in. What is the most likely species in that type of cover? (I'm not saying I always make the right choice, but if you know each bird's habits and habitat the chances are in your favor.) Is the cover light, heavy, wet, or dry? What is the dog doing besides pointing? Is his head high or low? Is the dog rock solid? I also watch my dogs' eyes. They convey to me what's happening on the ground.

Each species of game bird reacts differently on the ground when pointed by a dog and pursued by a hunter. A covey of Huns will stay together as much as possible and move in the direction of their flight destination. This may be right, left, straight ahead, or it may even hook around, but if you know the covey's previous movements and study the terrain for the birds' best escape route, and watch the dog's movements, you can usually figure out where the birds will flush. A covey of Huns flushes as a unit unless the birds are separated on the ground, and then they will flush in small groups or singles.

A flock of sharptails or prairie chickens spreads out, moving away when pointed to give themselves more room to fly. They often flush in singles and doubles. Sage grouse, when pointed, spread out from side to side, many times hooking around in back of the hunters. Sage grouse usually flush in singles. Once a covey of Huns or a flock of grouse are flushed and broken up, small groups and singles act quite differently on the ground because they are uneasy about not being together. This may be the reason singles and doubles hold better and hide using their camouflage instead of running.

With valley quail and the desert quail species, which I call western quail, I use the same hunting strategies with the dog, even though their habitats differ. Western quail like to have a view of their surroundings, and they will always see you before you see them. Any quail will run or fly from an unfamiliar noise or

Reading a dog's posture can tell you where the birds are.

movement, but western quail run because it's more energy efficient than flying and because the habitat is conducive to ground travel.

Valley, Gambel's, and scaled quail often congregate in large coveys numbering 60 or more birds. When I spot these quail on the ground, I give the dogs plenty of time to work the cover. By the time the dogs get to where I first observed the birds, the birds invariably have run and started to break up. The key to my method is to walk leisurely and give the dogs more time to work the birds, which helps to scatter the covey. When worked slowly, the covey has time to split up and divide into smaller and smaller groups.

Western quail do not fly or run hundreds of yards, nor do they leave familiar country. They are locked into a cruising radius with a much smaller range than other game birds. When followed, some quail flush, some fan out, and others run. Splitting up is a survival technique. A single bird, if captured, is a sacrifice for the survival of the group. Once out of harm's way, the birds start forming small groups and work toward an assembly area or back to the place where the whole covey first scattered. They also use the fastest routes and best ground cover to get together.

There are not many opportunities to capture on film a flush of Mearns' quail. Nor are there many chances for a double. But Sam Smith is doing just that.

Once the dogs point, the hunters should move alongside the dogs, walking at the same pace without stopping. After they pass the dogs, both hunters should flare out right and left, widening the space between them. When hunting wild birds with a pointing dog, the secret is to walk slowly and let your dog do its job.

THE SEASON DICTATES THE SCENT

As far as I'm concerned, every day in the field is a good day; however, some are more productive than others. Understanding how a bird matures and reacts to changes throughout the hunting season will lead you to more successful days afield with your dog.

Cover

My first consideration is the seasonal variations in cover type. The plant community goes from various shades of green to colorful hues to shades of brown as the season progresses. Agricultural crops are cut, foliage is lost, and shrub and grassland vegetation becomes parched. These patterns change my hunting procedure, and they change how the dogs perform.

During the early part of the hunting season, green foliage masks the scent birds leave. Dense woodlands and green vegetation such as sweet clover, rabbitbrush, sagebrush, among many others, can be so pungent that other odors are overwhelmed. Dense vegetation in forest and field locks bird scent into a small space. That means a pointing dog has to cover every square foot of ground to find scent, which is impossible. Visualize a small fire in high, compact, green cover. Little smoke is released because there is

Cover dictates how well game birds hold. Follow the direction of the dog's nose and that is where the birds will be.

no air movement, and what smoke is present is being blocked by vegetation and does not dissipate. Bird scent behaves in a similar fashion.

Weather

My next consideration is climate. North to south and east to west, you have got to know the territory. Is the country dry, wet, hot, cold or covered with snow? Daily weather patterns are influenced by the climate, and these help determine how, where, and when the dogs and I hunt.

No one knows conclusively how severely pointing dogs are affected by inadequate scenting conditions due to green vegetation or daily climatic changes, but I suspect that the amount of moisture in the atmosphere and the wind currents play a large part in pointing dogs not finding birds. Watering dogs often adds moisture to their nostrils and helps them scent better, and I am sure that any wind movement, no matter how slight, is important for dogs to pick up scent.

Birds

A bird's habits are dictated by its age, location, and surroundings. Its behavior on the first day of the hunting season is quite different than its behavior on the last day of the season. On average, most birds are still juveniles when the hunting season starts. Some are only half-grown — what I call peepers. The cryptic coloration of their plumage helps peepers stay alive, as their survival instincts tell them to freeze when approached. This can be great for a young dog or one still rusty from a long summer vacation.

The bird's age plays a role in the scenting equation. Young birds give off less scent than adults as a defense mechanism against animal predation. I have seen dogs surrounded by chicks and juvenile birds without knowing they were present.

Bird hunting across America can take you into beautiful landscapes.

David Foster, editor-in-chief of Gray's Sporting Journal, *scratches Winston's ear while waiting for the flush of a spruce grouse.*

I also enjoy evaluating why birds change their habits as they mature. Every game bird modifies its behavior as it develops and adjusts to variations in the environment. Some game birds change very little throughout the hunting season; some change dramatically. For instance, the Montana gray partridge season starts September 1 and lasts until mid-December. That's over a hundred days, and by the end of the season the juvenile bird's life span and life experience have each doubled.

In surrounding states, the gray partridge season opens around mid-September, which I believe is a more appropriate time. This gives young Huns two more weeks to mature, making them more challenging, faster targets. In Montana, I would rather see the first two weeks of the season removed and tacked onto the end.

As the hunting season advances and the birds mature, I change my hunting tactics. The dogs also adjust and approach birds differently. I might add that a smart, seasoned bird dog learns this on his own, without special training, but he has to be exposed to all of the changes in seasonal hunting conditions for this to occur.

Here is one example: My dog Hershey has learned to hunt sharp-tailed grouse differently as the season moves forward. Later in the year, sharptails may feed in more open country, such as short stubble or cut hay fields. When Hershey scents a flock of grouse in short cover, he points at a greater distance, works toward them slowly, and then points again. If a bird Hershey

is pointing raises its head and becomes visible to him, he will flatten out on the ground with his head stretched out.

By the time hunting seasons close, the birds are fully-grown. Adult birds use their senses to escape from danger, depending upon their eyes, ears, legs, and wings. When cover type, daily conditions, and the maturity of the bird are considered together, it definitely provides the hunter an advantage in knowing what to expect from the game birds. This combination also helps to evaluate a dog's behavior. If all three scenting disadvantages — lush vegetation, dry, calm weather, and young birds — occur at the same time, the chances of any pointing dog finding birds are greatly reduced. In northern parts of the country, this only happens at the beginning of the season. As the season progresses, these conditions diminish. Vegetation is down, there is plenty of moisture in the ground and in the air, and birds are fully-grown, giving off plenty of scent. This all works in the dog's favor, although the birds become educated as well, using their experience to scamper out

John Hughes examines a short sharp-tailed grouse. Watering dogs often in hot weather aids in helping to find birds in heavy, grassy cover.

Sometimes a canine friend needs a little help. John Cey helps his German short-haired pointer over a fence. My Brittany, Mac, waits his turn.

from under a point and bolt for cover on the wing. For me, hunting becomes better as the birds mature from peepers in September to rockets in December.

HUNTING HAZARDS

The anticipation and excitement of traveling to new bird hunting country brings out the best in hunter and dog, but we sometimes forget about the numerous hazards that confront these wonderful animals in the field.

Before I leave on a hunting trip, whether it's just beyond my backyard or at a distant location, I make sure I have everything necessary for a day afield.

Occasionally, I become so preoccupied with my own gear that I forget a few items necessary for my dog. To help out my sometimes-failing memory, I keep all of the essentials in one large container: water pans, bottles, forceps, combs, rope, leads, blanket, whistles, beeper collars, body protectors, duct tape, biscuits, and a complete first-aid kit. It's all about being prepared. Most dog hunting hazards can be avoided and many minor accidents can be treated in the field if the hunter brings the right supplies.

Experience has shown me that most problems in the field come from relatively few sources. Here are a few of the major ones.

Rattlesnakes

The rattlesnake is probably the most feared dog hazard. As a precaution, snake-break training can help. The best method, if you have access to it, is a veterinarian's snake aversion training program.

I train my dogs to avoid snakes in the field if the opportunity arises, and I do the same with porcu-

I train my dogs while in the field to avoid snakes. This is just one good reason to make sure your dog comes when called.

pines. Does it work? No guarantees. Does snake breaking with an electronic collar work? Some people swear by it, but I don't.

The best precaution is to avoid snakey areas, such as rocky places or piles of brush during warm weather. If the worst happens, keep the dog calm and get him to a vet. Don't try anything fancy yourself.

Porcupines

I consider porcupines more of a threat to dogs than rattlesnakes because my dogs have more contact with

Steve Claiborn holds Perk, my young pointer, after his first encounter with a porcupine. I remove the quills myself as soon as possible. He's a smart dog, and this was his last skirmish with a porcupine.

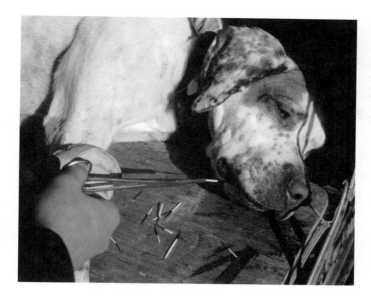

Perk calms right down while quills are being removed, and he's back hunting in minutes.

them. Many dogs seem to be attracted to porcupines, and with some dogs, not even training lessons or numerous ugly encounters seem to help.

If a dog is hit by a porcupine I work on him right in the field. It is important to pull the quills as soon as possible. High-quality forceps are a necessity — don't forget them! If your dog doesn't cooperate and allow you to pull them, then get to a vet.

Water

Always carry water for your dog in the field. If open water is available, beat the heat and immerse the dog in it. A dog's heat regulation system requires water, and there is no substitute for lots of it, even in cool or cold weather.

Even with snow on the ground a dog can use a drink of water.

Perk Perkins stops and waters the dogs while hunting scaled quail in the desert southwest.

Sore Pads

Use dog boots when necessary. Rocks, sand burrs, cactus, frozen ground, and steep slopes can cut or quickly wear down a dog's pads. For every mile we walk, a dog runs many, many more. Liquid pad hardener works well, too.

You also need to check a hard-charging dog's under-carriage. Buckbrush, rose bushes, stubble fields, cactus, and sharp rocks all play havoc on a dog's stomach. Hard-running dogs can quickly wear the hair and skin off their underparts. In some areas, a tummy-protecting vest is important.

Ben Brown attaches a stomach protector to his Brittany before hunting in desert quail country.

Cactus

Dogs can get stuck from all kinds of cacti. Always carry a good pair of forceps. They get the job done.

Javelina

In the Southwest, javelina can be dangerous for dogs. They seem shy and will often run away from you, but they don't exhibit any fear around dogs and can do a nasty job on an unwary bird dog. If you encounter some while hunting, call your dog in.

Burrs

Burrs in the fur are not a real threat to a dog, just uncomfortable. A small metal comb is all you need to remove them.

Seth Hadley removes cacti stickers from his Brittany Jasper.

Lynn Dawson combs burrs out after a day's hunt.

TAKING A TRIP

When traveling to a new area, I first decide what species I'm going to hunt. Then I research the bird — its habits, habitat, and the best way to hunt it with pointing dogs. I study distribution maps to learn where the greatest concentrations of the birds have been in past years. I call, write, or use the Internet to contact federal and state agencies involved with land use and hunting. Indian reservations, state tourism departments, chambers of commerce, sporting goods stores, hunting books, magazines, and local publications are all good sources for hunting information.

I pick an alternate location as a backup if bird populations have declined. Go where the birds are, not where they used to be. As the trip draws near, last-minute reports are essential. I call the most reliable contacts I can find for the latest information on bird populations and weather conditions. Be prepared to change plans if need be. I also set dates to coincide with the most favorable weather conditions in that region.

Ben's Dogs

Two Pups of the Same Color

Paddington and Leo were born in May 1975. As pups they looked like bookends. Their marking were so similar that I decided to keep both of them to have a pair of "twins." Both of their parents belonged to me and were outstanding natural gun dogs and bird finders. They had the genes that bird dogs are made of.

By the time bird hunting season started on September 1, the pups had plenty of pointing and backing under their collars. Every time I took them out for a training session, one would always outperform the other, but I was never sure who was going to be top pup on a particular day. They were so similar in their actions and hunting abilities that it seemed like they had just decided to take turns.

Now, of course, I don't believe they were capable of that kind of reasoning, but something was certainly going on between them. I loved to work them as a pair. They looked so much alike it was just a pleasure to see them run together. The one thing that bothered me was that as the two dogs developed, they spent a great deal of time hunting side by side, covering the same ground almost as one dog. So I decided to separate them.

When hunting alone or with other kennelmates, both dogs always performed to their full capacity. As the season progressed, both dogs started to show slightly different hunting techniques and retrieving traits, so I put them together again.

To this day, I'm not sure who was the best of the two, Leo or Paddington.

But when I did so they reverted to taking turns with who was going to perform best. Both dogs were highly intelligent and never did anything wrong when hunting together. But to this day, I think they enjoyed bamboozling me when I put them down together.

Winston: A Little Rambunctious

Winston is my second Brittany to be called by this name. My first Winston was the greatest bird dog I have ever had. This Winston is trying to be, but he is a little too rambunctious. As soon as I park the hunting rig, Winston knows I'm going to hunt, but it has never dawned on him that I have eight or ten other dogs with me. Naturally, Winston thinks he's top dog and should hunt first. Just as soon I get out of the pickup, he bangs his nose against the door of the kennel box and cries to get out.

Once on the ground, his beeper collar attached and turned on, he races off to find every bird in the country before the other dogs get out of their

Young Winston thinks he is my best dog, but he has a way to go.

compartments. He tends to be more interested in pursuing the hunt than in being sociable, although I must say that I find this is an attribute, not a fault. If he finds a covey of birds first, he holds as solidly as the Rock of Gibraltar.

But being too energetic can get a dog into trouble, like when not honoring another dog on point. Winston is a smart dog, but he can't stand being second fiddle when it comes to pointing. So Winston and I had several confrontations about his stealing another dog's point. For a while he played by the rules — until he conjured up a new trick.

When backing another dog, he'd wait until I walked by him and then move, making a half circle to steal the point from the side. As I have said elsewhere in the text, I do not yell or discipline dogs until after the birds have flushed. After watching several of these same maneuvers, I clipped a lead on his collar when I walked by and made him stay.

Winston is a wonderful dog, and even though he is highly energetic, I would never try to break that spirit. He finally learned to be more patient on his own, although I can see in his eyes that he would love to take charge, because he still thinks that he should find all the birds. But you can't fault a dog that has that much enthusiasm.

BEN O. WILLIAMS is a noted photographer, author, bird hunter, and dog breeder. He is the author and photographer of *American Wingshooting* and *Hunting the Quails of North America*. His photography and writing have appeared in many prominent sporting magazines including *Grays' Sporting Journal, Retriever Journal, Pointing Dog Journal* (for which he is a columnist), and *Shooting Sportsman*. He lives along the Yellowstone River outside of Livingston, Montana, with his wife Bobbi, fourteen Brittany spaniels, and two English pointers.